Andreas F. von Recum

Motorcycle Dreams

Editions Dedicaces

MOTORCYCLE DREAMS

Book cover: Courthouse, Bellefontaine, OH.
The author or someone in his family shot all photos in
this manuscript, unless specially acknowledged in the caption.

Published by:
   Editions Dedicaces LLC
   12759 NE Whitaker Way, Suite D833
   Portland, Oregon, 97230
   www.dedicaces.us

Library of Congress Cataloging-in-Publication Data
   Recum, Andreas F. von
      Motorcycle Dreams / by Andreas F. von Recum.
      p. cm.
      ISBN-13: 978-1-77076-397-5 (alk. paper)
      ISBN-10: 1-77076-397-X (alk. paper)

Andreas F. von Recum

Motorcycle Dreams

Lasting Childhood Impressions

During a reception given for my seventies birthday, my grandson Evan drove a tricycle on our backyard patio, round after round. He was three years old, but maneuvered his tricycle around party chairs and flowerbeds with great precision and care. I offered to move these objects out of his way but then I observed that he actually enjoyed steering around them. While watching him my own childhood came to mind. At that age I had no tricycle or bicycle, not even a wooden scooter, with wooden wheels and a bicycle bell on its steering handle like the one my kindergarten friends had. But I had the burning desire to own one.

Evan's Delight, 2009.

Towards the very end of WWII, German-speaking civilians fled from the Russian occupied parts of Eastern Europe to find refuge from the war destructions and the Soviets' wrath. Many thousands fled to those parts of Germany that were occupied by the western Allied Powers, Great Britain in the north, France in the west, and the U.S. A. in the south. The interim German government assigned those refugees into temporary accommodations in homes of local citizens. Since my parents lived in a large, rented 12-room townhouse apartment, the Bavarian government had seized six of those rooms for three refugee families, one family for every two rooms. One of those families had fled from Poland-occupied Silesia. The middle-aged head of that family, Mr. Hausmann had taught agricultural technology at technical colleges back home in Silesia and he succeeded to be hired right away into a similar position in our county since not enough local men had returned from the war to pick up teaching again. Commuting to the various colleges in our county, Mr. Hausmann drove a brand new motorcycle of the Bavarian Motor Works (BMW) with a sidecar. To protect himself from the weather, he wore a new, good smelling leather coat. It reached down to his calves and squeaked with every step he made.

Russian Replica of The 1937 BMW R71

(Permission by John Landstrom, Blue Moon Cycle, Inc.)

Based on what I remembered I recently studied BMW web sites and determined that Mr. Hausmann's motorcycle resembled a model 1937 R71. The attached sidecar was most likely from Steib. To verify what I remembered and what could be possible, the web archive informed me that the R71 was built from 1937 until 1941 mostly for military purposes.

There was no civilian motorcycle production during the rest of WWII. The first postwar model was a one cylinder R25 produced in 1950. I remember people in the later fifties driving those R25 motorcycles, but they did not resemble at all Mr. Hausmann's rig. Since my story about Mr., Hausmann happened during the end of the forties, his rig must have been a Model 1937 R71. Why was that so important to me?

This photograph shows a brand new rig of today, as it is manufactured and sold by a Chinese company and distributed worldwide. It is a replica of the original rig as it was built by BMW until 1941. Mr. Hausmann's rig was an original BMW product hidden somewhere from 1941 until the end of WWII, hidden from governmental confiscation until 1945 when it became legal again to buy and own motorized vehicles.

At that time, I was six or seven years old and the rig's beauty smote me. Some of its details I remember vividly. The motorcycle and sidecar were of black, shiny color with a white pinstripe on the side of the gasoline tank, along the fenders, and around the sidecar. I also remember the two, tractor-like rubber seats. They felt so comfortably sprung and so soft to sit on them. The motorcycle had a black number plate on the front fender (not shown here), and a black tonneau, buttoned over the entry into the sidecar, to keep the weather out.

Hardly anybody could afford to own a car in those early postwar years, not even my parents. The German government had confiscated most motorized vehicles before the end of the war. They were to help with the last, desperate war efforts of the German military. Only few people rode small, prewar motorcycles for commuting, but I had never seen a big motorcycle with sidecar like this one. Mr. Hausmann was very particular about it and kept it spotless at all times. There was plenty of room in our garage to keep this precious rig protected from the weather and from vandalism. A military-grey dusting rag was always spread over the driver's seat.

There it stood over night in its immaculate condition. Occasionally, I would sneak into the garage, carefully close the garage door from the inside, climb onto the big rubber seat, and pretended to drive the rig. I especially remember that with the tip of my left foot I could reach down to the gear shifter, and how difficult it was to place my right foot onto its foot peg underneath all the linking rods that connected the sidecar to the motorcycle frame. I also remember that the owner had to push the rig rearward out of the garage into our cobble-stone-paved courtyard. There he would kick down a starter leaver at the left side of the motorcycle. The engine would start right away, and a muffled, low pitch exhaust sound, boobb-boobb-boobb-boobb, would tell that the engine had started idling. Mr. Hausmann was always dressed in his mahogany-colored leather coat that reached down almost to his ankles. He would swing his right leg over the motorcycle's saddle, sit down on it, re-arrange his coat, and drive the rig quietly but majestically forward and out of our courtyard into the street. There was no "toeff-toeff-toeff-toeff" as we were used to hear from the small, two-stroke motorbikes of those days, nor the roaring of the Harley-Davidson motorcycles or their Japanese imitations of today. Image and sound of the BMW motorcycle brand imprinted permanently in my head as something extraordinarily desirable. "When I was to be grown up", I always fantasized, "I would drive one like that," while some of my little friends dreamed of driving a fire engine in their later life.

Starting My Motorcycles
First, A Moped Will Do

Eight years later, I had to commute daily to a high school in the neighboring town of Lauingen at the Danube river. At first, I drove a bicycle since there was only a short drive of 5 km (3 miles) on a well-shaded, hardtop bicycle lane. I actually liked riding bicycles and even enjoyed that daily ride. I often raced it all the way with other classmates. After such races, when I arrived home breathless and covered in sweat, my mother would conclude that my ride to school was too strenuous for me. On my 16th birthday and because I reached the legal age to ride a moped, my parents bought a used Herkules moped for me. The *Nürnberger Hercules Werke*, a pre-war manufacturer of good motorcycles and bicycles made the moped's frame while its 50cc two-stroke engine was manufactured by *Fichtel & Sachs*. The entire vehicle looked like a more solidly framed woman's bicycle and therefore, I was not very happy with it.

Zündapp Moped about 1955 (Web Photo by Rolf Granath, Sverige)

Six month later, my parents exchanged it for a new, more reliable moped manufactured by another highly respected motorcycle company of pre-war times, Zündapp. My new moped, just like the one I now found on the web, was more solidly built even though it still had only a 50 cc engine, which, however, was made by Zündapp itself. In my mind, this was the top moped make and I considered it my Cadillac.

Although I was convinced that I did not really need this luxury means of transportation (none of my school mates had one), I quickly enjoyed every day's rides and the sudden freedom and advantage it provided to me. I could ride wherever I wanted. Sometimes I left home in the morning, but then, on the way to school decided to take an unexcused absence and drive through the hills and woods of our beautiful southwestern district of Swabia. Around noon, when classes had finished, I arrived back home and, I still believe today, I aroused no suspicion at home.

Because my school performance declined (and the moped was only one of my many distractions), my parents transferred me into a boarding school in Eichstätt, a beautiful, small town 80 km (50 miles) northeast from my hometown in the Bavarian district of Lower Franconia. There I stayed for three years until I graduated from high school. The moped gave me the ability to drive home on weekends, or instead to explore the very romantic countryside north of Eichstätt in the Frankish Alp.

During one summer, I spent the six weeks school vacation in Munich, where my older sister Cissy lived. To get to Munich was a 100 km (62 miles) trip on country roads, a trip that took four hours with the moped, which traveled at a top speed of 25 miles/hr. I had been offered a volunteer job near Munich to which I commuted from my sister's apartment every day. Riding the moped through Munich's downtown traffic took about one hour to get there. This amounted to a lot of driving that summer, but the tiny little moped engine never, ever, complained, or needed any repair.

When my oldest brother Dieter started college in a university town far away from home, and when he needed a means of transportation, he bought a brand new Adler 150cc motorcycle. This was a real motorcycle and impressed me, compared to my little moped. Already its name (translating into Eagle) had an important ring to me. Perhaps I thought so because my father often talked about his elegant Adler Sports Coupee from Triumph, that he drove before the war. When my brother came home one day, I was eager to try his new motorcycle. He said, however that "one day I would be able to have my own motorcycle and then I could ride it". "Without a motorcycle drivers license", he said, "I would not even be legal to drive it". My argument that I had been driving my moped for some years now did not convince him of my applicable skills. A year later, he came to visit with the famous NSU Max, a 250 cc street motorcycle that had made its name winning street motorcycle races in the fifties. Of course, I was not allowed to drive it either, because, he said, it was "too powerful for me to handle". With it, he made a tour to Spain the following summer. Somewhere there he contracted a serious diarrhea, had to spend a week in a hospital, and then rode back home, still feeling very sick. When he was back, his interest in motorcycles had waned.

Starting in the mid fifties, peoples' living standard had improved and they were now looking for a cleaner and more comfortable means to get to work. This desire, especially of women, gave birth to the family of motor scooters. By the late 50', the scooter varieties had gradually increased adding engine sizes up to 250 cc.

Then "micro" cars evolved. They were not based on the vast prewar experience building expensive cars for the wealthy. Rather, a new class of car owners had to be served: the low-income factory worker who needed inexpensive transportation with some better protection from the whether. Famous ones were the German brand "Messerschmitt". Its cabin and Sachs 200 cc, two-stroke engine allowed for the transportation of two grownups sitting behind each other, just like on a motorcycle. It resembled an airplane cockpit, a comparison, which was not too far fetched since the manufacturer had been in the business of building fighter airplanes during the war. With a further increase of the living standard, the Messerschmitt improved with better and faster engines, with windows that could be opened, and with two wheels in the back. The Isetta, an Italian design was manufactured by BMW using a 250 cc, four-stroke, one cylinder BMW R-25 motorcycle engine. Its cabin also provided seats for two grownups but they were sitting next to each other. The Isettas were originally running on three, and later on four wheels.

Recently, when I drove home on US 64 West coming from Richmond Virginia, I saw a motorcycle shop sitting right next to the northbound lanes of the interstate and immediately before the exit ramp to Covington. Its name looked like Knick Classical Cycles. In its west-facing window there was an Isetta exhibited. It reminded me of the current design of mini cars such as the French made -- and Mercedes Benz distributed -- *Smart "For Two"* that I recently saw in Marietta.

A little Mercedes Benz of the 21st Century, 2009.

It seems, that my brother Dieter, who studied electric engineering at that time, had been able to afford an Isetta and one day he came home with it. This car opened the entire front side for access and Dieter graciously allowed me to sit in it, next to him, and to adore his little wonder, but "I could not drive it", he said, "since I was still too young and without a driver's license."

Then, during the late fifties a number of small, low cost cars became available. There was of course the Volkswagen (VW), and also others of *Borgward, Lloyd, DKW (now Audi), Fiat, Citroen, Renault, Morris*, and an English Ford, to name a few of the more popular European makes. They provided protection against the rain and the cold and they had more seating and storage capacity. They also started to fit the budget of the Germans who experienced their *Wirtschaftswunder* (economical miracle) that evolved to the astonishment and perhaps envy of the neighboring nations.

When the German military was reestablished in 1955, my older brother Dieter joined it immediately and was now able to afford a "real" car with four wheels and a capacity to seat four people of postwar weight. When he came home to visit, he drove a Volkswagen (VW) called "Beatle" in the USA. It had a military grey color, the only car model and color that could be had from the Volkswagen Werke for a number of years. An 800cc, air-cooled engine propelled the Beatle. It was developed by Porsche and was mounted in the rear of the car.

I did not even ask permission to drive it because I was too proud to risk another rejection, but soon thereafter, my father started to have a car again and I learned to drive in his car. As much as I enjoyed driving cars, my fascination, however, stayed with two wheels, although they rapidly declined in numbers on the streets of the beginning sixties.

The Norton Experience

After graduation from high school in 1961, I sold my moped to another high school student and hitch hiked to Edinburgh, Scotland where I spent a year. To earn my keep there, I worked as a delivery boy for a small, street corner grocery store downtown, near Circus Place. All day I loaded grocery orders into the store's boxy Vauxhall van and delivered them to wealthy customers throughout the town of Edinburgh. Slowly, I learned to find my way around the center of the city and I earned enough to cover my living expenses, to attend English classes of the Berlitz School in the early morning, and participate in rehearsals for choir and brass music at the University of Edinburgh in the evenings. There was even some money and time left to purchase and operate a used motorcycle.

In those days, Edinburgh impressed me as a very romantic city. The real and the foe gothic architecture in sand stone dominated the city everywhere and created an atmosphere of lasting value. The sand stone surfaces exhibited weathered colors from ochre brown to light gray. High rainfall generated an additional mossy green on the weather-exposed building sides. Most of the time, cool winds chased white clouds over light blue skies, unless it was raining. These watercolor combinations in their many shades were a daily treat for my eyes and mood. The three weeks of Edinburgh International Festival in the late summer transformed the town into a giant theatre of the finest arts and music of Western Civilization. On Downtown's Princes Street and the nearby castle, hundreds of flags would fly in the invigorating wind and concerts were given every day and all day long in many of the public buildings, some free of charge. During my lunch hour, I would often attend a concert in a nearby church on the south side of Princess Street.

The delivery tours during the day and the motorcycle rides after work hours allowed me to explore the downtown Royal Mile and all its beauty. Its atmosphere captured my phantasy. The city planners' had succeeded to hide the downtown Waverley Rail station so that the roaring of incoming Diesel trains, was filtered visibility and noise effectively by Princes Street Park. Thus, Edinburgh retained its romantic image. To me, it was a shining example of how to maintain a vigorous, lively, beautiful, and exciting downtown. I found myself to be the most fascinated tourist absorbing the cultural atmosphere of this town.

In Great Britain of those days, 15 years after WWII, motorcycles were widely used as the common people's means of transportation. Motorbikes, as they were called there, were considerably less expensive to ride as compared to even the smallest cars such as the Morris Minor which was built from 1947 onwards until 1971 while it had become a symbol of "British-ness", or the Austin Mini that had just come out in 1960 and of which well restored examples are still around in 2010.

The British weather allowed biking almost every day of the year, especially if one had water resistant clothing to protect from always-possible rain showers. There were many motorcycle manufacturers in the United Kingdom of those days, such as BSF, AJS, Matchless, Triumph, Norton, and many others which I cannot even remember. The usual engine sizes ranged from 100 cc to 750 cc.

Robert Bonner, a native of Ardrossan near Glasgow at Scotland's West Coast was my roommate for 3 months. We lived together in a two-room flat above a fish-and-chips shop in St. Leonard's Street, very near the center of town. Robert was a

14

student in chemical engineering and a passionate spectator of motorcycle racing. He owned, what I believe now, was a Norton Manx single-cylinder 500 cc motorcycle, which he rode to the many local motorcycle races throughout the year. Mostly, however, he worked on the motorcycle's mechanics and appearance. Motorcycle parts were usually lying on the carpet of our joint living room, waiting for cleaning, surface re-finishing, or re-assembly. Because our carpet had a natural, dark-brownish color the many engine oil stains did not show that much.

With very little money to spare and having no knowledge of British motorcycles, I was strongly influenced by Robert's allegiance to the Norton brand and that was how I stumbled into my first motorcycle purchases. Advised by Robert, I first bought a Norton ES2 500 cc single-cylinder motorcycle, and Robert taught me the basics of its care, repair, and riding. Unlike this beautifully restored bike I recently found on a Web archive, mine was a tattered commuter motorcycle. To my taste, it was too loud, its ride was too rough and choppy, and its engine created so much vibration that essential parts kept braking off and had to be welded back on or temporarily wired on or affixed with electric insulation tape. Within a month, the dealer kindly took it back and let me choose instead a Norton Dominator 99 with a 500 cc vertical twin engine, just like the one shown below which I also found recently in a web archive. It was in mint condition, and riding it felt like sitting on a plush sofa rather than a three-legged, wooden milking bolster.

Norton ES2 500 cc single-cylinder (Web: Ronald Saunders) and The Norton Dominator 88 of 1959 (Web Site Photo).

I knew nothing of the background of this motorcycle; it might have been a few years old when I bought it and I do not remember its mileage, but it was in excellent esthetic and mechanic condition, ready to be enjoyed. Its frame was supposedly designed for extra comfort and safety of the driver, rather than for winning competitive sports. Its 500cc twin engine had a nice humming tone.

There was only minimal vibration within normal driving ranges and the motorcycle ran smoothly through all its gears. The gears shifted effortless with my right foot, the first one upward, and the other three downward. With this motorcycle then, I explored the Scottish/English Border Country, a landscape that spoke to me in its romantic layout of rolling hills, where heather and fern covered treeless hills and where single sheep strolled through the growth, widely dispersed over the landscape. Since I had relatives on the English side of the border in Corby, near Carlisle, Cumberland, the motorcycle allowed me to visit them frequently on weekends.

One day, a well-to-do lady to whom I regularly delivered groceries, asked me whether I would take her visiting niece with me for a motorcycle ride. She was a lovely but shy 16-year-old girl and seemingly eager to ride on the motorcycle. We took a two-hour trip to Queens Ferry northwest of Edinburgh. She sat behind me, relaxed and apparently fearless and made it easy to balance through the many curves along the road. There was no opportunity to have conversations with her -- our wax-cloth-and-cork construc-ted helmets, and the noise of the headwind prevented that, but I enjoyed her warm body leaning against my back. The trip was a great experience for me and perhaps for her, too. A week later, when I delivered grocery to that same household again, I offered another pleasure ride, but the girl had already gone back to her hometown somewhere down in England.

On another day, Robert suggested that we ride to Glasgow to attend a college rugby game between the traditional archrivals, Glasgow and Edinburgh. He suggested that we take his motor-cycle, with me riding on his back seat. In spite of his racing fascination, he was a diligent, and courteous rider and he influen-ced my motorcycle driving habits for the rest of my life. Still, I was terrified sitting behind him without any controls in my hands. I sat there tensed up and not trusting his judgments. During that trip I concluded, that I did not enjoy riding the back seat and I have avoided it ever since. Nevertheless, I learned the very best in motorcycle riding from Robert. He was always keenly aware of the weather and road conditions and was attentive to the road surface ahead of him. He often warned me about objects lying on the road or loose gravel at the side of the road. He was a defensive driver, always anticipating that others near him might endanger him. On the other hand, he did have a racing driver's dare that puzzled me at times. One day I said I would go to buy crash bars for my motorcycle. The bars would be mounted on the motorcycle's frame to protect the engine and the rider's legs. Many people used them, but he was adamantly against them. "They would bend my frame and render my motorcycle worthless after a crash", he said. I argued that they could also save my legs from major injury. "Your legs will heal but the motorcycle will not", he said in an authoritative tone, intolerant of backtalk. Although I did not buy into his argument, I also did not buy the crash bars. In hind site and looking back at 50 years of motorcycle riding, I would have never needed them.

One weekend during the winter, my seventy years old aunt Mary at Corby Castle invited me to stay with her for the upcoming weekend. I was very fond of her and always glad to visit. Although it was a rainy day in Edinburgh, with near frost temperatures, I mounted my solo motorcycle with a novice's naiveté and started the trip that normally took 2 hours. At first, everything went fine, perhaps because I was a timid driver and drove slowly with maximal attention to the road conditions. That day, there was no traffic on the road, which should have been a warning to me. When I entered into the Cheviot Hills near the English border, the road was suddenly covered with black ice which made me slow down even further. With a speed of about five miles per hour, I reached a tiny bridge that arched upward over a creek, just like the wooden bridges on Japanese paintings. In slow motion, the motorcycle made a low side out of the driving direction and slid on its side, wheels first, into the grassy ditch. Since everything happened in slow motion, I could easily get off the motorcycle while it slid away. Nothing was damaged. However, because the grassy ground was covered with a sheet of ice I could not lift the motorcycle back up into an upright position or push it back onto the road because I slid away myself.

After trying for some while, a small, chocolate colored Morris Minor delivery van approached slowly. A man with a giant, red-brownish handlebar mustache climbed out of the van and helped without asking questions. "Cold day, isn't it?" he said more as a statement than a question and without expecting an answer. Together we succeeded to bring the motorcycle into an upright position, push it to the other side of the bridge, and set it up on its side stand. "Drive carefully!" the man said with an east coast Scottish brogue while he climbed back into his car. His mustache was frozen over by then. The hardness and shortness of his pronunciation sounded like that of legendary, US, syndicated, radio commentator Paul Harvey. "Good day!" he uttered while he drove off.

Since there was no visible damage to the bike or to me, and because everything was still in working order, I mounted the motorcycle with "shoogely" knees and rode through the rest of the hills in walking speed with my feet sliding on the road surface. I arrived at my aunt's little house by midnight. Unbeknownst to me, she had also invited her nice, a lovely 18 year old girl and they had been sitting and waiting on me for many hours. My aunt was kind and understanding at my delayed arrival, but her nice was visibly angry and kept protesting that she did not appreciate my aunt's apparent matchmaking efforts.

These two Norton motorcycles were my first big ones, and I needed to learn the most basic things about their maintenance and repair. In those days, I did not know about the existence of motorcycle repair manuals, as they are so readily available nowadays. By trial and error then, I learned to do as many things as could be done with a kitchen-drawer tool collection, which included a few wrench sizes, a screwdriver with a badly worn blade, a pair of pliers, waxed wrapping paper, and sticky, black electric insulation tape. After a few times of tuning and balancing the carbureting, I learned to hear the individual pistons and could tune them to the same pitch and intensity. When there was a significant oil leak from the motor block I learned to replace the cylinder head gasket. Gaskets were not readily available but Robert had taught me to cut gaskets out of waxed sandwich wrapping paper and to coat them thinly with ball joint grease. When I had inserted the homemade gasket and tightened the bolts of the cylinder head, one of the bolts broke off, leaving a stump

18

inside the engine block. I had no means to remove it and Robert was not available for advise or even help. He was out of town on spring brake. I took the city bus to the motorcycle shop and asked for help. "Bring the motorcycle and we will fix it," the man said with a kind smile, indicating that this was a common problem not only for beginners. Following his suggestion, I pushed the partially disassembled motorcycle from my home, through downtown Edinburgh all the way to his shop at the east side of town. It took me two hours to get there. Within half an hour, the mechanic had removed and replaced the bolt, and it took me two more hours to push the motorcycle back home. This was a harsh lesson to learn as to how much bolts can safely be tightened.

My First Sidecar

After WWII, solo motorcycles, and motorcycles with side-cars were the workhorses of the British working class, since their operation was more affordable then that of cars. In addition, the relatively mild weather on the British islands allowed for motor-cycle use almost all year around. Many different sidecar models were built in Great Britain to fit all sorts of needs. There were delivery boxes as well as sidecars for one, two, or even three persons who were sitting in line. I always loved to see them on the road.

When my time had come to move back to Germany and to start my veterinary medical education in Giessen, I had accu-mulated too much luggage to hitch hike back with it or take trains. Instead, I purchased a used sidecar and had it attached to my Norton motorcycle. It was a nice and clean, well-preserved, one-person sidecar. I even fit into it myself.

I do not remember any details of the age and the make of the sidecar, but Tony Cox, a friendly service man of Watsonian-Squire Ltd in England today, determined from the pictures, which I had e-mailed to him in 2008, that it must have been a 1960 Watsonian Monaco Classic. "The sidecar would originally have had a 10" steel wheel," he said, "with a push-on Watsonian wheel trim".

The sidecar was in exquisite condition, had no mechanical problems, not even scratches, dents, or rust on its well-kept body or its convertible roof. My friend, the motorcycle mechanic in Edinburgh attached it to my motorcycle with four linking rods while I was watching.

The Norton Rig, 1962.

To me it looked easy as if there was nothing to it. The mechanic insisted that I also purchase the two necessary wrench sizes so that I could make adjustments when necessary. Within a few days, I learned to drive the rig and to cope On the web I found a history of the Watsonian sidecars and there it was reported that by "1955, 160,000 sidecar outfits (were) on the road – 50% of them were Watsonian." with a few near-accidents that stemmed from the rig's directional stubbornness. Eventually I gained the feel for steering the rig safely at my will. No adjustments needed to be made, or better said; I perceived no need to make adjustments. There was nobody who told me how the rig should be running and I was happy with the way it did.

Then I loaded all my belongings onto the rig. They included four suitcases, a Grundig tape deck recorder with about 50, 6-inch tape wheels, a bag of dirty laundry, two satchels with books and correspondence, and a trombone in its case. Everything had to fit into and onto the sidecar, the seat behind me, or strapped on my back; and they all could be accommodated. My roommate John Mitchell watched in unbelief.

This luggage had to fit into the rig, 1962.

The trip home to Bavaria took two days of driving, interrupted only by one night on the ferry from Dover to Oostende (The Netherlands) where I slept in a bunk bed on a lower deck, while the rig was fastened to the floor in between cars on the upper deck. Other people on the ferry said to me next morning that they could not sleep because a heavy windstorm had made them sick, but I had slept through it.

To drive the rig (or combination, as it was called in the UK), all the way from Edinburgh, Scotland to my hometown Dillingen at the Danube River in Bavaria, was a fascinating but exhausting experience. To prevent me from falling asleep I constantly calculated my driving speed converting it from miles to km hundreds of times throughout each day.

Passing through Belgium covered the most mind-numbing stretch, 150 miles of flat and abundantly green terrain. French poplar trees, planted in lines left and right along the roads, where the only objects that poked out of the landscape. On the way, I passed by some famous cities including Bruges, Gent, Brussels, and Leuven. Every one of those towns would have been a worthwhile interruption for my driving, with plenty of educational sight seeing, but I had no time since I was focused on getting home. My back hurt badly most of the time. Scooting back and forth on the two-person, bench seat helped a little to alter my back position. It also helped that I stopped for 15 minutes rests every two hours. Then, I moved my luggage out of the sidecar, climbed into it, closed the hood over me, and shut an eye or two. Eventually, I arrived safely at my parents' home. The total trip time was 30 hours traveling 1,200 miles on the road.

During the two weeks I spent at home, my older brother, Dieter, by that time a lieutenant in the German Army, came to visit while he was on vacation leave. To my amusement, he was eager to test-drive the rig. I hesitated: "You would have to learn to drive a rig," I said, "since it behaves so very different from solo motorcycle riding." He countered that he was an experienced driver of tanks and other large military vehicles and that it would not be a big deal for him to drive this little rig. I faked great concern that would prevent me from letting him drive it on a public road. Eventually I insisted to sit on the back behind him while he drove it over a soccer field, and he agreed. He was so eager to try it. There was a soccer field not far from our home. Sure enough, when I suggested to take a right hand curve somewhere in the middle of that field, he kept on going straight until I pulled on his right arm to help him change direction. Of course, he did learn quickly thereafter that a rig had to be actively steered through the handlebar. I would call this incident now "the rare triumph of a younger brother".

The long hours of continuous travel at highway speeds had been more stressful to the motorcycle and the sidecar then they were built to handle. Two weeks later, on my way to my new university town, Giessen in the State of Hesse, a dozen of spokes broke out of the rim of the sidecar wheel and it collapsed. Stranded on the narrow gravel strip at the side of the German autobahn of those days, I detached the sidecar with the two wrenches (which the sidecar dealer had urged me to buy). It was detached within minutes. A tow car came by and picked up the sidecar. The truck driver knew of a nearby motorcycle repair shop and transported it there while I strapped my two suitcases onto my back and the rear seat and continued the trip to Gießen on the solo motorcycle. In those days, there were no special alterations made on the motorcycle to accommodate sidecar driving since they were designed to accept a sidecar. Consequently, I could easily switch over to riding the solo motorcycle.

Then, a few days later, on my way to visit my second sister in Frankfurt, one of the two engine cylinders seized while I was driving at highway traveling speeds on the left, fast lane of the German Autobahn. The motorcycle could have had a high side crash -- coming to an instant halt with the motorcycle flipping and I tumbling off -- but due to a clever Norton design of a rubber-mounted clutch, the clutch disengaged instantly and the motorcycle coasted to a safe stop on the left side's gravel strip. The rubber mounts of the clutch saved the motorcycle and me from total destruction. A car driver behind me madly blew his horn. He must have been angered by my drastic slowdown on the fast lane, but by God's Grace, no one was hurt. He passed by without even slowing down. When there was no upcoming traffic, I rolled the motorcycle onto the gravel strip on the right side and waited. Hours later, when the engine had sufficiently cooled down, I was able to start it again. At a very slow speed and with an annoyingly loud knocking noise of the pistons, I returned to Giessen on backstreets.

Local motorcycle shops were not willing or able to repair this British motorcycle. One must understand that by 1962 almost all motorcycles as means of transportation in Germany had been replaced by cars. Motorcycle dealers had to diversity by selling bicycles, sewing machines, or washers and dryers. Motorcycles, the mules of postwar transportation had become outmoded. Even in Great Britain, Norton and other British motorcycle manufacturers struggled through the sixties and most of them folded in the seventies. I had never seen another British motorcycle in Germany while I studied there in the sixties. Only a small number of motorcycle brands survived that crisis including BMW in Germany, Moto Guzzi and Ducati in Italy, and of course Harley Davidson in the USA.

For the seized cylinder, someone recommended a small company in Hamburg that dealt with cylinder heads and cylinders. I phoned the company and was instructed to bring the cylinder block and both pistons. Encouraged by this possibility, I dismantled the engine, stuffed the cylinder block and the two pistons into my brief case, and hitchhiked 274 highway miles to Hamburg. Due to this travel mode, I had no control over travel times and arrived there on a Saturday afternoon. The company had just closed for the weekend. Seeing me standing at the door, someone had pity on

23

me, let me in, honed out the two cylinders right then, fitted new piston rings, and sent me back home. The whole process lasted less than an hour and I paid 50 German Marks, the equivalent of $12 at that time. The next two days I spent on the road back to Giessen, hitching many different rides, often only for little stretches. In order not to miss any riding opportunity, I slept the night under a highway overpass. The whole journey took 5 days, which was the entirety of my spring brake. It took another day to re-assemble the engine, while other students stood around me and watched. There were bets going on behind my back whether I could restore the engine's function.

When the sidecar was repaired a month later, I rode the motorcycle 200 miles to that repair shop and re-attached the sidecar there. Traveling back to my university town on the re-assembled rig, I had a mixed feeling of pride to have everything working again, and disappointment, that everything took so much time and money neither of which I could afford during my veterinary medicine studies. It turned out that the costs of riding and maintaining the rig, unfortunately, had greatly exceeded my modest student budget and free time. Although I earned some money by trimming poodles and serving on people in a diner of the nearby Schiffenberg Castle, it was not enough and sadly, I had to sell the rig. For a while, I was without a vehicle and devoted all my time to the study of veterinary medicine. I also learned to know a wonderful young co-student at the university, Gudrun. She had one opportunity to ride with me on the bike, and when she later had agreed to marry me, I had concluded that she was not against motorcycle riding.

The Honda Interlude

Ten years later, during the seventies the western world experienced a renaissance of motorcycle riding as facilitated or even instigated by the clever Japanese motorcycle industry. At this time, there was not so much a need for low cost transportation but a desire for motorcycle riding as a sport. Suddenly half a dozen of Japanese motorcycles of good quality appeared on the market to entice a new type of customer: the pleasure rider.

Horst and Uta "hot-rodding" in Colorado, 1974.

Although our children's motorcycles came already in hotrod style and fashion, the Japanese street motorcycles of the seventies were initially following the postwar style and technology. I actually liked that style because I could comfortably sit upright on those motorcycle.

With my wife, Gudrun and our four children we had moved to Fort Collins, Colorado, in 1972 to attain some specialty education in veterinary surgery. On weekends, I had to drive 60 miles to Denver, Colorado for an internship at the Denver General Hospital. Since there was no convenient public transportation and since we could not afford a second car for my commute, I bought a new 1973 Honda CB 350, two cylinder motorcycle. This was to be my means of transportation for the three years at Colorado State University.

After I had adjusted to the gearshift being on the left side of the motorcycle, and that the gears shifted in opposite direction (as I was used to shift on the Norton motorcycle), it became a pleasure to drive this mid-sized motorcycle in the Colorado Foothills. It was perfectly smooth and comfortable to ride for local commuting and short pleasure drives, but it was not designed for prolonged rides at interstate travel speeds of 70 miles/hour just like my previous Norton Dominator was not either.

My helmet and goggles of the fifties and sixties were still in style (see also on the photo of my Norton rig). The helmet was made out of cork covered with a black paper or a papery, black plastic foil, which, for a short time held the rain water off, but was not very durable. The goggles sat tightly over my eyes and nose and contained real glass lenses. Consequently, they were scratch resistant and raindrops on them were so close to the eyes that they did not hinder vision. In addition, they protected the eyes from the drying out effect of the Colorado wind. Long-sleeved gloves kept the cold from creeping into the jacket sleeves, a must in Colorado.

The new little Honda CB 350, 1973.

The Brand Of My Dreams
The R50/5

When we decided to stay in the USA, I exchanged the Honda for a brand new, 1973 BMW R50/5. In my thinking, this long-term acquisition should stay with me the rest of my life. It was in the classic black color with white pin stripe, just like the one that stood in my parents' garage 30 years ago. Additionally, a Vetter Windjammer fairing shielded the driver from the wind, and two Vetter hard shell saddlebags at the rear of the motorcycle were big enough to hold a helmet and my work satchel. Here I was now, riding my thirty year old, secret dream: a BMW motorcycle. It was such a good feeling to fly on it down the highway to Denver. There was a minimum of vibration at highway speeds. It handled the long highway trips with ease, purring along on the little-used US 87, humming like a well-oiled Singer sewing machine. When I stood next to the idling motorcycle, its engine sound was just like I remembered it from my childhood, a low pitch, muffled *"doobb-doobb-doobb"*. When I rode the motorcycle, the sound underneath me was different. I could hardly hear the low pitch, muffler modified exhaust sound that bystanders would hear and like, but now I heard the klicking of the tappets, which I needed to accept as "normal".

There were some other outstanding characteristics of BMW motorcycles. The two pistons that protruded from the sides of the engine block gave the motorcycle a low point of gravity and their positioning allowed for good engine cooling. Those cylinders did not reach upward under the gasoline tank, and the heat of the engine did not rise toward the rider's trunk and buttock as is so pronounced in the Harley-Davidson and big Honda bikes. Finally, this motorcycle, like all BMW motorcycles had a low-maintenance driveshaft. There was no driving chain with its *"rrreshshshsh"* driving noise and therefore, no need for frequent chain maintenance. The boxer engine and the driveshaft were treasured design principles in those days (also of Moto Guzzi), which, in the mind of many, made BMW a hallmark of motorcycle engineering into the 1980ties.

The motorcycle moved with us to Northville, Michigan where we lived for the next three years. My job was downtown Detroit, at Sinai Hospital and I commuted with the motorcycle the 18 miles of dense town traffic every weekday, except when there was snow or ice on the road. My work at Sinai Hospital and Wayne State University was so intense, my young and growing family so wonderful to be with, and our three-acre hobby farm so demanding, that there was no additional time or interest left for pleasure riding through the Michigan country side. Three years later, we moved from Northville to Clemson situated at the Foothills of the Blue Ridge Mountains of South Carolina. Since both, the motorcycle and I originated in Bavaria, we both loved the hill country. Unfortunately, the distance from my home to my Clemson University office was less than half a mile and too short to even get the engine warmed up. Again, there was very little opportunity to ride it for pleasure. Although the climate for motorcycle riding was just right much of the year, I had so little time for the motorcycle in that phase of my life that I never even thought of making good photographs of it.

Still, there were some memorable motorcycle moments. Once, we had our van at the Dodge service station in Seneca, about 5 miles from our home, and we received the call to pick up the van. Gudrun was pregnant in her last trimester with her sixth child and, since we had no second car at that time, we took the motorcycle to ride there. When we arrived at the service station two mechanics stood at the garage entrance and could not help grinning at us three on the motorcycle. We would not have thought much of it because there had been many transportation needs which we solved this way, but years later, when we brought the car to the station again, the two mechanics could not help but grin again and they told us what they thought was a funny picture, we three on the motorcycle back then.

When my oldest son reached the age, when he eagerly wanted to drive the motorcycle, I was afraid to let him learn riding on this big and powerful motorcycle, and I sold it with a bleeding heart. The new owner was barely 18 years old himself. As I was told years later, he did not appreciate the value of that particular road motorcycle and he used it for off-road mud slinging with his

28

buddies in the foothills. I often wished I had kept that motorcycle. I would have liked to drive it now in my retirement. It had the perfect size and performance for me, the gentleman rider, and I would have taken good care of it.

My son Derik took my advice and started to tinker with a much smaller motorbike, and when he came home from military basic training in Germany, he bought a Japanese motorcycle to fulfill his transportation needs for a little while. Years later, again, when he came back from another military assignment in Germany, he had bought a Harley-Davidson.

Derik had become a diligent and careful driver and I was proud of him. Because Harley-Davidson offered a special deal for US soldiers serving in foreign lands, my oldest son-in-law Greg also bought a Harley-Davidson. Both invited me at different occasions, to test-ride their motorcycles and I felt honored to do so. Unfortunately, my first impressions were not favorable to that make. Both motorcycles were too heavy for me to handle and to hold upright.

Furthermore, the seating position was low, forcing my knees and hips to be strongly angled and located in front of me, with the foot pegs high up so that I had to lift my legs and feet in order to change gear or brake. The engine was unnecessarily loud and the entire motorcycle vibrated so heavily at idle and at all driving speeds, that my hands numbed. Perhaps I was to old for this size motorcycle and its specific pleasures.

Once I had pushed these heavy motorcycles off their center stand and running, they handled nicely and I lost a little of the fear to drop them. Commanded by my lack of security and the motorcycle's noise and size, I needed a full lane's width of road. It felt to me like driving a mid-size John Deer tractor. I had to admit that I would never, ever want to master a Harley-Davidson and I wondered what attracted my sons to own theirs. There must be something to the Harleys that fascinates the majority of US motorcycle riders of today.

Test-riding Greg's Harley-Davidson, 2008.

Of course, as one can easily see on this photograph, that I did not have the right attitude toward this motorcycle make and my observations were made from a insensitive perspective of a narrow minded BMW fan.

The K100

March 8th, 2006. To make a long story short, I was ready again to own and ride a motorcycle of my own. I was within two month of retiring from my academic career, was physically and mentally still able to handle a midsize motorcycle, and was looking forward to spend time fooling with a BMW motorcycle as my next occupation. Because my legs were no longer strong enough to keep a bigger motorcycle upright, I decided to look into buying another rig. On the web, I found two different rigs for sale within neighboring states. A BMW K75 with a smaller sidecar was advertised somewhere north of Chicago, and another one, a BMW K100, was located near Indianapolis, only half the distance from us, and so I planned to visit the closer one first.

Developed in the end seventies, the K motorcycles represented a new design concept for BMW in order to compete better with giant touring motorcycles of American and Japanese brands.

Breaking with the long hailed BMW tradition of a two-cylinder, air-cooled, boxer engine, the K-motorcycles came onto the market in 1983 like a revolution featuring in-line cylinders lying horizontally. They were water-cooled; sported electronic fuel injection, and were fitted with power-assisted brakes. This new motorcycle type was hailed to be especially sturdy, reliable, quiet, with minimal vibration and long-distance endurance. The rest of the K-motorcycle attributes were reported to be in line with BMW's tradition such as high quality, and high cost. Initially, the K75 and K100 models were essentially the same, except that four cylinders with 1000cc capacity propelled the K100 and three cylinders with 750cc capacity powered the K75.

Now I had the vexing questions: should I stick with the famous BMW history of the boxer engine concept which I had loved since my childhood or should I try the K concept which was by now in its 23 years of existence? If I were to choose a K motorcycle, which one would best suit my needs? To find answers I studied the web thoroughly. There I found abundant information on the advantages and disadvantages of the airhead (boxer engine) and the K motorcycles, more than was helpful to make a choice, but reading all this information increased my urge to buy a motorcycle, any motorcycle, and now!

Picking a Rig

My youngest daughter Elsa (as my best supporter of the motorcycle idea), her husband Jonathan Meyer (a BMW fan), my wife Gudrun (in charge of our finances and anticipated partner in travels with a motorcycle), and I (the eager customer) drove to Indianapolis. We pulled an empty utility trailer behind our car, just in case we would decide to buy a motorcycle with sidecar on that very trip.

The K100 rig stood in Cicero IN, in front of Greg TenBrook's house and it was a "looker". This big and very compact BMW K100 model, so called flying brick, was built in November 1984. It was dressed up with the upper part of BMW's LT fairing and one saddlebag on its left side. A rather spacious, English sidecar was attached to its right side. Since this K100 model was no longer built for sidecar use, it had been modified for sidecar riding by a previous owner, Greg Baumgardner in Springfield, OH, who then sold it to Greg TenBrook, the current owner. The rig was freshly painted in a loud Volkswagen cyber green.

The BMW K100 Rig, 2006.

Greg Baumgardner had bought the K100 in 2001 from a man in Columbus OH of whom he only remembered that he lived at Wilson (Bridge?) Road, and he had bought it with the intent to combine it with a sidecar.

For that combination, he also had bought a sub-frame from somebody in West Virginia. The UNIT SIDECARS LTD in England had manufactured that sub-frame especially for K motorcycles. From a person in Wisconsin he had obtained a used sidecar, a Watsonian Monaco Classic, which needed major restoration first. For that restoration, he imported a windshield, the top of the boot, and a seat from England.

Through the UNIT sub-frame, the sidecar (also called "chair", "hack", or "outrigger" among the rig driving folks) was rigidly attached to the motorcycle using four official links. In order to increase the attachment strength, he added another link each to the front and to the back attachment points of the sidecar frame, adding up to six links.

The leading link fork (Worthington 2007).

He had also replaced the K100 standard front fork with a leading link fork made by EML Engineering in the Netherlands (see photo), allowing the motorcycle with the attached sidecar to turn curves with less effort. The original BMW single piston front disk brakes were replaced with double piston Sumitomo disk brakes, normally used by the big Yamaha motorcycles. They fit the modified front fork and lent more braking power to the greater weight of the rig.

Furthermore, upon recommendations of the sidecar litera-ture, the motorcycle's tires had been replaced with car tires of a flat profile supposedly to provide better road contact and straight forward driving stability. A very comfortable, leather-lined Corbin dual seat replaced the standard, plastic covered BMW seat. A BMW hard shell saddlebag, matching the LT fairing in color and style, was attached to the left rear. Since there was not enough space on the right side, between the motorcycle and the sidecar, a metal frame was attached to both, the right rear of the motorcycle and onto the sidecar fittings. It provided a platform for a reserve gasoline tank or for luggage placement, and it gave additional stability to a trailer hitch.

Someone had painted the rig in cyber metallic green (2005 VW 57166C LG6V) and the sub-frame and attachments were powder coated in black. A trailer hitch with the necessary wiring was firmly attached to the sidecar fittings. The former owner Greg Baumgartner sold the rig to the latter owner Greg TenBrook in approximately 2004. The latter drove it for a year and then sold it to his father in Tennessee who (through his son) sold it to me a year later, March 8, 2006. The latter Greg had only exchanged the sidecar wheel (normally10 inch wheel) to a 12-inch, four-lug Wal-Mart trailer wheel suitable for a standard 12X4.80 trailer tire. Both together were comparatively less expensive than the original British sidecar tire alone, and they were readily available at Wal-Mart stores. The overall diameter of this new wheel and tire, however, was a little too large and the tire had rubbed against the rear attachment bolt of the sidecar fender. The latter Greg, therefore, had ground that bolt thinner to allow for a free spin of the tire. The space gained by grinding was only a few millimeters and the danger of accidental blocking the tire with road dirt wedged between the bolt and the tire remained always in my mind. Both previous owners told me, that they now drive other rigs: The former Greg combined another 1986 K100 with a wider EML sidecar, and the latter Greg, as we saw in his garage, combined a Honda Goldwing motorcycle with a modern, more comfortable looking sidecar.

We liked the offered rig and worked out a reasonable deal. Because I was afraid to drive an unfamiliar rig for 200 miles from one state into another in 35° cold weather of early March, Jonathan's father had lent us his standard 6X8 ft. utility trailer. At first, it seemed that the rig was about two inches too wide for it. A one-ft. railing around the trailer deck was limiting. When we removed the motorcycle's left saddlebag, and the mudguard off the sidecar wheel, and when I had placed a pile of three, 2" thick boards on top of each other and under the wheels, then the rig fit just barely onto the trailer.

In this elegant tow, we drove our acquisition to its new home in Worthington OH. It would now become my retirement occupation. Three more months of administrative work were still to be completed at Ohio State University, but thereafter, I thought, I would have unlimited time to devote to the rig and its mainte-nance and riding. The latter Greg had given me a handwritten sheet of instructions on what worked how and why, and it became a useful guide for the following weeks. Unfortunately, a driver's manual did not come with the motorcycle, but a year later, my BMW service shop gave me a used driver's manual for my K100, which provided answers to some remaining questions of proper motorcycle operation.

Short Trips in Ohio

Owning a touring rig, I knew in advance, would mean two things for me, the young and yet inexperienced retiree: First, I would have to spend much time for repairs, upgrading, and beautifying the rig, and secondly, I would want to explore Ohio from the top of the motorcycle's seat. Most of the repairs needed to be done when problems occurred, only a few projects could be planned ahead of time. I had built a shed housing the rig and the car garage would be available for greater repair projects.

Planning for riding tours was altogether a different matter. Such tours needed careful mental preparation of my wife Gudrun and my daughter Elsa, who both feared the widely bemoaned dangers of motorcycle riding but they were also a little jealous of the time I would not spend with them. Mapping out a travel plan, and careful timing it to fit the family calendar was therefore essential. Finally, I had to pick days when sunshine was predicted since I had no raingear.

Sightseeing in Ohio also presented some challenges. Unlike some other states where great outdoor spectacles lure the tourists, Ohio has only few such attractions that would interest me, a culturally starved tourist. Also, they are spaced far apart from each other along the state's boarders. The greater center of the state is flat and very suitable for field crops such as corn, soya, and sod farming but with little excitement for sightseeing motor-bikers. Columbus sits in that flat land in the center of the state, and from there, it takes at least two hours of interstate travel to reach the geographically more varied peripheries of the state in any of the four directions. Central Ohio was rubbed flat by millennia of moving ice and rubble in pre-historic times. Beyond that center, there are a few beautiful sites. Mind-stimulating varieties of land-scapes with hills and valleys, forests, and prairie appear in the southwest counties of Clermont, Brown, Highland, and Adams. Similarly, the Appalachian foothills southeast of Ohio present exciting landscapes and interesting historical sites such as the Hopewell Indian mounts, or the well-visited Hocking Hills and its neighboring counties to the east and south. In fact, all counties in East Ohio that are wedged between Interstate -77 and the Ohio River have fascinated me.

Last, but not least, there is the famous Holmes County in the North East of Columbus. For my southern German geographic and cultural background Holmes County was the most pleasing area to visit. Its scenic topography of gentle hills with intermittent farmland, farm buildings, and forests, and its farming methods reminded me of the Southwest of Germany, where I grew up and where the Amish people originated. It reminded me also of the early fifties in Germany, when horses did the heavy farm work and when farms diversified, deriving income from farm and forestry crops, gardening, and from those farm animals that could be raised on that land: Chickens, geese, pigs, goats and sheep, dairy cattle, draft horses, mules, and donkeys were penned up around the farmyard creating the noises and smells that were reminders of my youth. They had generated my childhood dreams to become a veterinarian. I would never have thought that such sensations would please me in my advanced years, but they did. Touring with my rig allowed me to see, hear, and smell all this, unaltered by closed windows, air conditioning, and radio sounds, which I would have in a car.

Marcia Schonberg in her book "Ohio Travel Smart"[1] suggested interesting and useful categories for best tours in Ohio. Each of these categories focused on general topic or preference for sightseeing: Arts & Culture, Nature Lover's, Family fun, on the Presidents' Path, and Underground Railroad Stations. My sightseeing by motorcycle, however, focused less on museums, culinary attractions, details of battlefields, or family fun, but rather on the beauty of the countryside and how man uses it for dwelling and farming, which I could fly by and enjoy.

At first, I took short trips of two to four hours around Columbus with the main goal to learn to master the rig. Southwest trips, staying south of I-70, touched the towns of London,

---

[1] John Muir Publications, Santa Fe, New Mexico, 1998.

Washington Court House, and Circleville. Northwest trips above I-70 brought me to Marysville, Bellefontaine, Kenton, and Marion. Both these directions led through an eternity of crop farmland, mostly on perfectly straight and flat county roads that carried very little traffic. While the corn and sod fields rushed by me, I had much time to listen to the performance of the motorcycle's engine and to fight my back pain. After those trips, I grew a little disappointed about the lacking environmental attractions and I frequently wondered why I bothered to have a rig. Also, I became worried about the noises of my motorcycle's power train and the stability of my lower back.

The next tours concentrated on smaller circles east of Columbus. Such trips, staying south of I-70, led to Lancaster, Logan, New Lexington, and Zanesville. All four downtowns have their architectural beauty and interesting history and I marked them for later, more intensive visits and sightseeing.

From Lancaster I remember a monument at the junction of Main and Broad Street. It honors General William Tecumseh Sherman in bronze and life size. He is celebrated there as the preserver of the Union. Although his victory over the South was an impressive military one, the hail on the plaque sounded peculiar to me: Having lived 25 years in South Carolina there the Union general Sherman is condemned as the brutal destroyer of southern economy and self-esteem.

Other trips, staying north of I-70, brought me to Newark, Coshocton, Mt. Vernon, and Delaware. Those trips revealed beautiful stretches of road, winding through hills and valleys, passing by bogs and prairies that seemed to be left for the enjoyment of the nature enthusiast. They appeared to me suitable for motorcycle tourism and yet, I often wondered why I did not see many more sightseeing motorcyclists. But then, I was retired and drove on weekdays and during normal work hours, while most motorcycle riders were probably working for an income and could only do their pleasure riding in the evenings and on weekends.

37

So, I searched for further traveling routes east of Columbus, as they will be described in more details in other chapters below. My youngest son-in-law Jonathan often joined me on his 1985 BMW R80 motorcycle, His companionship helped me to overcome the boredom of the first travel hour. Since we did not have modern telecommunication equipment, we could not actually converse while driving. We followed each other silently but talked during short rest periods every hour or two. Jonathan was the perfect companion and pathfinder – his good map reading and memory allowed for efficient travel on predetermined routes, and he seemed to like similar aspects of our tours as I did.

As one can imagine, the long hours of driving a rig provided much time for thinking and I had often questioned myself what I was actually doing? What was the profit of owning an expensive motorcycle, and what was the benefit to my soul? Gudrun often asked "What is it that you like when you drive for hours to nowhere." Did God want me to indulge in this self-pleasing hobby? I never came up with an immediate answer or solution; perhaps I did not want to be stuck with the obvious answer, but I observed that many rig owners, alone or within their sidecar brotherhood buddies arranged for sidecar tours for sick children. Sick children may enjoy such detractions from their shut-in hospital lives, while rig drivers may derive good feelings from their kind acts.

The Challenges of an Older Motorcycle

When I bought it, the K100 motorcycle was in a good operating condition and esthetic appearance considering its 21-years of age and I was grateful for all the good care which previous owners had invested in it. Yet, it became clear to me, that I, like they, had to do constant repair and replacement work to keep it in the same safe driving condition as they did. Some or much of it, I hoped, I could learn to do myself. First, I missed friends with motorcycle maintenance experience who could advise or even help me. Second, I had no well-stocked workshop of any kind. I had a toolbox with some generic tools from my prior biking life, and luckily, those tools were metric and useful for the minor repairs and adjustments on this motorcycle. Then I discovered that Jonathan, besides adoring almost everything German, he had a specific BMW fetish. He owned two, and later even three BMW cars and, in addition, the previously mentioned 1985 BMW R80 motorcycle. Besides his official title as my son-in-law, he volunteered as my driving partner and maintenance collaborator.

With time I found many things that needed to be adjusted or replaced and I pondered, what would require immediate repair and what could be assigned to a maintenance schedule for the coming year?

Nowadays, information of all kinds of repair and maintenance for all kinds of motorcycle makes and models is freely available on the web. With little effort, I found an abundance of specific information for the BMW K100, even for my model year 1984. Most advice came from lay people who must have been owners of K100 motorcycles. Among that information was also a list, provided by Don Eilenberger of November 2001 with the title: "K-Motorcycle Buyer's Guide". He must have been a professional BMW service man. He recorded the most likely problems to be anticipated for the K100 model and how they could be diagnosed and repaired. This list became my guide to recognize what went wrong with my motorcycle and what needed to be fixed now or eventually. In addition, I purchased two different, second hand service manuals to help me understand the technical terms, to find pictures of the items of disrepair, to locate them at the motorcycle, to find the appropriate tool, and to attempt fixing the problem.

The Haynes Service & Repair Manual[2] was more suitable for the gentleman driver, who has a limited understanding, few tools, and no facility to do sophisticated repairs (this characterizes me). The *Clymer BMW Service, Repair, and Maintenance Manual*[3] provided exhaustive details and it was designed more for the well-equipped repair shop. Now, the Ellenberger's list I read every now and then. According to it, almost everything that Ellenberger predicted to fail did fail and needed repair on my motorcycle. Actually, eight out of his 13 topics occurred on my motorcycle while I owned it. These repairs consumed much time and some money. The other five listed problems had either happened with previous owners, had not happened yet, or were not relevant for my specific motorcycle model. I will not describe any of those problems here but some major additional problems took me a long time to diagnose and then to repair.

Some Electrical Tasks

During the very warm months of May and June of 2007, some annoying issues developed slowly with the motorcycle. A few times the engine would unexpectedly cut-off while I was driving but I could bump start the engine immediately and continue to drive again. Then, once or twice in the morning I could not start the engine with the start button but only by pushing the motorcycle downhill. What was the reason for these malfunctions?

---

[2] The Motor Bookstore - Car and Motorcycle Repair Manuals, 404 Newtech Court, DeBary, FL 32713-4841 U.S.A.
[3] Clymer Publications c/o Editorial Director, 9800 Metcalf Avenue, Overland Park, KS 66212-2216.

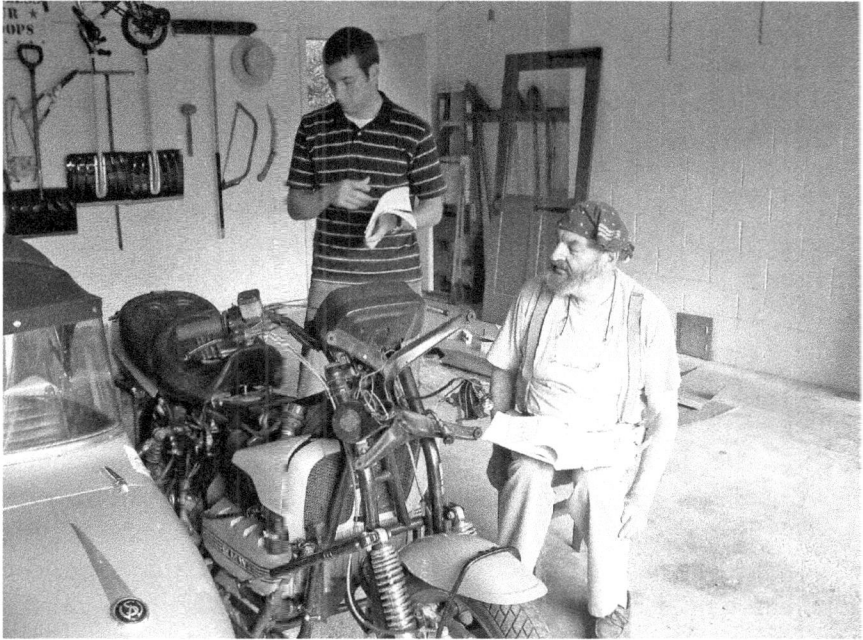

Jonathan helps me with the electrical challenge, 2008.

Thinking that a low battery charge level could be the culprit, I recharged the battery many times overnight, not realizing for quite some time, that a fuse located within the charging cable was blown. Then, during a spin around the block, one very warm night the head light was flickering and so was the sidecar's sidelight. When I stopped to investigate the problem, the headlight and instrument panel lights did not turn off anymore after I had removed the ignition key. Finally, the headlight quit altogether. All the while, I could jump-start and drive the motorcycle.

There was enough battery power since all other battery-fed features worked. Suspecting a short of the electrical circuit somewhere, I decided to inspect the entire wiring harness (which I had done before with two of my former cars). To approach the main harness and its connection to the relay box, the fairing, and the gasoline tank had to be removed as well as the battery. The picture above shows that situation: the front of the motorcycle is naked and the sidecar sits to the left. The main wiring tree is exposed and I am sitting next to the motorcycle with the repair manual on my knees. Jonathan holds some extra website pages and explains what we could test next.

41

There, located under the gasoline tank, I found a bare wire section, connecting the ignition/light switch at the handlebar to a power saving relay in the relay box. The wire insulation had melted away and fused with the insulation of neighboring wires forming with them a big glob of insulation material and wires right in front of the relay box. Some of the bare wire I could free from others, hopefully yet undamaged wires. I cut the culprit wire section at its both ends and replaced it, bypassing the wire and insulation material clump. I also replaced the power-saving, generic relay, the corroded ignition switch at the steering bar, and all fuses that I could find, including the one in the battery charger cable.

After I had recharged the battery using a new cable with a new fuse, everything worked admirably then. My self-esteem rose measurably, even though I had approached this problem empirically and not in a prospective fashion as a good engineer Like Jonathan would have done. Some time later I read reports on the overheating tendency of the K100 model, telling me of yet another, well-known K100 problem that I had faced with my motorcycle. The cooling advantages of the boxer engine had been abandoned and replaced in the K100 with its tightly packaged 4-cylinder engine sitting right underneath the gasoline tank. Its heat cannot but rise up to the tank and the cable tree immediately below it. While repairing the wire connection, I should have thought of some heat shielding or thermal wrapping around the cable tree to avoid future insulation melts, but I did not think of it then.

After the fairing and the gasoline tank were re-attached, the rig was ready again for a test drive, which proved the following functions to work again: headlight, sidelights, starter button, and ignition key. The whole repair process took five full working days of labor and my constant worry that I might not be able to find and repair the problem and that I might have to give up on the motorcycle because it had too many costly problems. Eventually however, I wondered whether I should charge myself for 40 hours labor as a veterinary fee of $250/h, or as mechanic for $80/h, or as a volunteer for a pat on the back. Of course, the latter was the least expensive. It pleased Gudrun the most, and so I went for it. Amazingly, I spent as little as $50 for parts purchased at the nearby NAPA car parts shop.

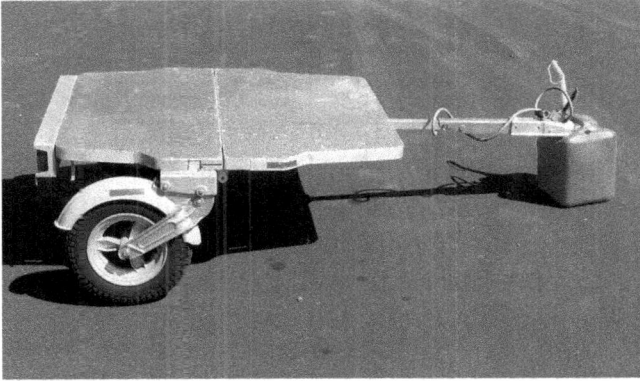

Gudrun inspects the Little French-made trailer, 2010.

Another wiring job was already waiting in line. A friend had offered me his little utility trailer suitable to be pulled behind a motorcycle or small car. For $100, I took it. The trailer had a round, cylindrical, 7-pole connector, whereas the motorcycle was fitted with the standard, flat, 5-pole connector like my car and my big utility trailer. I had a difficult time to assess, which wire needed to be attached where, and after fooling with it for two days without making progress, my son Horst and Jonathan, both educated and practicing engineers, attacked the problem systematically. They found a web site that had various connectors and converters and wiring diagrams. It took them less than an hour to find the right connections between the motorcycle and the trailer. Then every light on the motorcycle and trailer worked, as they should. One of the added challenges was that the wiring harness of the motorcycle connected to the sidecar also, and a separate switch, unbeknown to me controlled the sidecar lights.

Then I registered the trailer with the county agency and obtained a license plate necessary for proper road use, if I ever was to use it. The total cost of this venture was $120 for the trailer and electrical parts and $45 for the trailer registration. One day, I thought I might buy a lockable toolbox and mount it on the trailer surface. A year later however, having used the trailer not even once, I sold it on my daughter-in-law's garage sale for the same price I had invested in it. Beyond the fact that I did not need it, it also appeared to me as flimsily made and dangerous for the type of speeds the rig travels, especially if it were loaded with luggage.

A Long Test Ride

On Friday September 21, 2007, I was ready for a sight-seeing trip to the southeast of Ohio. The plan was to see how far I would get and how the rig would hold up. I had planned for an over night stay when necessary. I traveled I-70 east towards Wheeling. At Hendrysburg, I turned south onto SR 800, which turned out to be a beautiful road winding gently through hilly country with lots of interesting scenery.

Romanesque Church in Barnesville, 2007.

In Barnesville, the highest incorporated town in Ohio, I stopped for something warm to drink and eat and made a photo of the rig in front of the First Presbyterian Church. Built in 1903 in the Arts and Crafts style it looked (Richardsonian) Romanesque in its red appearing but polychrome sandstone. The building reminded me of Martin Luther's Hymn "A Mighty Fortress is our God". The architect might have thought of the image of the Christian congregation finding refuge from the liberal and perhaps even hostile influences of the society around them. Ohio has five Arts & Crafts churches in this stone from a quarry near Mansfield. The adjacent trees, here shown in autumn colors, camouflaged the fortress's appearance, but you might still see my little green rig in front of the building?

Further south, down the road, in Woodsfield, I turned onto smaller township roads that led westward over a branch of the Wayne National Forest. Narrow roads in excellent condition wound in tight curves along steep ridges. Left and right, exciting scenery of woods and pastures draped over hills and filling small valleys. It was the middle of the day and there was almost no traffic while I rode southwest until I reached SR 60. It led me north to McConnelsville. There, on the lawn of the Center Park I took a 60 minutes nap to relax my hurting back. When I woke up, an active farmers' market had surrounded me but I seemed to be in nobody's way.

Continuing the trip along SR 60 north, I reached Zanesville and turned back onto I-70 westward in the direction of home, where I arrived 10 hours after I had started there. The weather had been excellent with permanent sunshine, a temperature between 60 and 78°F and without any significant wind. The motorcycle performed well over the 300 miles trip. There were no apparent difficulties with the engine working an average of 4,000 rpm for 9 hours.

The motorcycle was actually in much better shape than I was. I was exhausted and suffered from annoying back problems. My back hurt continuously throughout the later two thirds of the ride and reminded me of my long trip in 1962 from Edinburgh in Scotland to Dillingen in Bavaria. Although the current motorcycle was much more comfortable and the trip through the southeast of the Appalachia much more exciting, the European trip was on a much smaller motorcycle and sidecar, and the landscape more monotonous for a whole day's distance. Yet, the back pain was identical and most uncomfortable. Was it the sitting position, the engine vibration, the constant tension of all back muscles, or my counter-steering to prevent the rig from pulling to one side or the other? Who knows? Perhaps it was all those factors combined.

Due to a mild engine vibration within the narrow range of 3,000 to 3,200 rpm (as read on my motorcycle's faulty speedo-meter), the right mounting post of the front fairing's rear end broke at the site of the upper motor mounting bolt. The post hung loose from the fairing for a little while and then it fell off. It had broken off because it was designed a little too short and held the fairing under constant tension. A few days later, I replaced the lost post. I bought an angled aluminum strip for $5, drilled holes on both ends for the mounting screws, shaped the top and bottom ends into a right angle, and bolted them into their place. At the same time, I contacted the BMW shop for a genuine replacement part. They looked at the motorcycle, decided that my original post was a custom made part and that they would not have anything like it. They also confirmed that my "contraption" was good enough for government work and inspection. In the South I learned a word that described this type of quick fix, but my last employer, the Dean of Veterinary Medicine at the Ohio State University, warned I that I should not ever use this term in public.

Coming back to the quick fix, I believed, that the vibrations would eventually generate a crack in the aluminum strip at either mounting site. Yet, the total materials cost was $8.00 and well worth its while.

Noises around the Front Brakes

The last Saturday of October promised to be a beautifully warm and sunny day and it enticed me to travel through some of the northwest of Ohio. Starting on SR 33 not far from my home, I drove northward to Bellefontane, turned onto CR 508 north to Kenton, turned onto CR 309 westward to Marion, and turned onto SR 23 south toward home again to complete the circle. The countryside was always flat and most monotonous giving me much time to contemplate again on what I was doing with my time and skills.

I covered 165 miles in little more the 3 hours. As noted on all previous trips, the road surfaces were excellent throughout and the average travel speed was 55 miles/hr. After about one hour, my lower back started hurting again, and after about two hours of intensive sunshine on my black helmet, my attention diminished drastically. In spite of that, I noticed that my front brakes emitted a faint metallic ringing when braking and a scraping noise persisted for a while after I released the brake.

Much time was invested then in fixing the brake, or better said, in trying to figure out how to fix it. Jonathan's deliberate approach would have been to read instructions before he would lay hands on tools and the brakes. Although this was often a more time consuming approach it always turned out to be the more efficient one. Since he was not available I started out with my empirical methodology.

The noise came from the front disk brakes and was not new to me. I had already planned for some time to check them out. So, the following week, the last days of October I started to service the front brakes. It turned out that the caliper on the left side was not centered well over the rotor disk and the rotors scraped on the inner housing side of the calipers. In addition the mount of the front fender was dangerously close to the brake caliper and may have interfered with the latter's function.

I removed both front calipers in order to clean and check them for proper function of their pistons. This repair led to a protracted sequence of events that lasted all November and most of December. It turned out that the calipers were not original (BMW) parts and none of the local BMW shops wanted to touch them. The calipers had the name SUMITOMO imprinted in their aluminum cast housing. Both former rig owners (Greg and Greg) explained to me per e-mail that the original BMW calipers had not been powerful enough for the rig, and furthermore they had not fit into the leading-link fork that had been installed by them. Only after repeated prodding, they remembered vaguely, that the calipers may have been from a 1989 Yamaha FZR 1000W motorcycle.

It took me weeks studying the web and calling Yamaha service shops repeatedly to verify the motorcycle make and the model year that used my type of SUMITOMO caliper. Then it took some more weeks to receive the seals that would fit my calipers. Three times, I had to return what had been sent to me before a set of piston seals finally fit. To re-assemble the caliper was relatively easy but bleeding the break system without special tools was a little more challenging for me. My BMW service shop completed that task. Was this repair necessary? I believe that the brakes functioned afterwards as well as they did before the repair, but the noise associated with the brake alignment was gone. Again, I felt the urge to congratulate myself for this success, but my humbleness prevented me from celebrating this achievement publicly.

By now, it was December 13, 2007 and the weather was less amenable for longer drives. On short drives around town, the rig ran like a charm without abnormal noises or performances.

with good road holding, and with good braking power as far as I could tell.

Throughout January, February, and March 2007, I was supposed to teach a course at the University and I would have commuted with the rig whenever possible, but then, not enough students enrolled and the course was cancelled. This lack of student registrations deprived me of a good reason to take the rig out at least once a week. I was restless, and often visited the motorcycle in my shed to check the battery, and let the engine idle a little bit. When March arrived, the rig and I were sufficiently charged up and ready to tour the country again.

Tuning the Linkage

One of my constant worries was the rig's tendency to pull to the side instead of straight forward. During short fun trips around town and on its in-town highways, I had to counter-steer all the time the rig's tendency to drag to the left. Especially, side-to-side unevenness of the road required particularly forceful counteraction. The motorcycle preferred to follow lateral unevenness downward toward the left or right, instead of staying with the road's longitudinal direction. I had to force steer in the straightforward direction. Also, side or crosswinds required forceful counteractions. This demanded much energy from my arms and back and could be responsible for my lower back pains. I did not remember so much steering problems with my first rig and so I blamed my current, heavier rig for these directional challenges. Consequently, I always drove slowly and overly cautious throughout the first year. At the same time I wondered: could the technology of rig driving still be so archaic and primitive in our days?

Again, the web contained much related information. There was a helpful German book out of the fifties on the engineering principles of sidecar driving, and there were many other recom-

48

mendations on the how-to of sidecar attachment, and then there were blogs, many of them providing more or less useful answers from-the-hip on sidecar related issues. Much of the year 2007, I played with the motorcycle's linkages to the chair and how I could optimize the rig's road performance. Unlike the simple linkage of my first sidecar in the early sixties, this one was much more complicated. Because, for unrelated reasons I had to disconnect and then reconnect the sidecar to facilitate two major repairs of the motorcycle's drive train, I had much opportunity to experiment with different connection settings.

As described earlier, the motorcycle had a special, custom-made sub-frame to accept linkages from the sidecar. The sidecar, in-turn consisted of a frame onto which the chair was mounted. There were two main anchorage points on the left side of the sidecar frame (see arrow on the front one of those points in Figure on the left). From each anchorage point, three rods reached over to the right side of the motorcycle and anchored on the motorcycle's sub-frame and engine block. It had taken me some initial courage to start fiddling with these connection rods; actually, my son-in-law Greg Broecker, visiting me on furlough, got me started.

Upon some web surfing, I found the following four recommendations for optimal tuning of the sidecar-motorcycle linkage:

1. **Toe-In of the sidecar:** provides effective steering assistance and 1.0 to 1.6 inch is recommended
2. **Lean-Out of the motorcycle:** effectively reduces pull to the right, and an angle of 1.0° is recommended.
3. **Lead of the sidecar wheel:** is mentioned theoretically to help in steering but no settings are recommended.
4. **Trail of the front fork angle:** is appropriately provided by the design of the special front fork of the motorcycle and cannot easily be adjusted any further.

Recommended Attachment Angles (AVR, 2008).

The literature said that motorcycle lean-out; track width, and sidecar toe-in affect driving and steering properties the most. With all these parameters and measurements in mind, I disconnected all linking rods except the lower front one that had a swivel joint but I loosened it. To prevent the motorcycle from falling while I adjusted the angle (since the motorcycle had no center stand) I propped it up with short boards in the front and the back. Then I set the motorcycle's leaning. The literature prescribed 1.0° to the left, and relative to the vertical axis. To make sure that the motorcycle was truly leaning 1.0°, I measured the lean-out angle with a neat little electronic digital angle gauge which carpenters use nowadays, and which someone on the web kindly recommended to me for this use. By means of its magnet, I attached it to the brake rotator disk of the front and then the same place on the back wheel assuming that the rotors are positioned normal to the wheel axle, and thus to the ground floor. This recommended, small degree of leaning, away from the sidecar is called motorcycle lean-out, a term that makes good sense. By this lean-out, the motorcycle would have the tendency to turn to the left, which counteracts the sidecar's drag to the right. Those two forces need to be balanced diligently to have the rig pull freely straightforward.

To guide me with the next adjustments, I positioned the sidecar to stand about parallel with the motorcycle. I laid two aluminum 2x4 C-posts longitudinally on the floor: one of them flanked the motorcycle's left side; the other one flanked the sidecar's right side, such that the post was laid parallel to the side of the rear wheel of the motorcycle and the other parallel to the side of the sidecar wheel. Thus, I had two longitudinal reference lines in driving direction, one for the motorcycle, and one for the sidecar. The track width of 46 inches was measured on a transverse from the center of the sidecar hub to the longitudinal along the motorcycle's side. This track width is supposed to influence the ease of steering. It is defined by the width of the sidecar and how close the sidecar is attached to the motorcycle. In my rig, the sidecar width had been fixed by the sidecar manu-facturer and could therefore not be adjusted. Regarding the closeness of the sidecar to the motorcycle there was only a tiny little play of an inch or two, which turned out to be unimportant. Actually, the distance I measured was within guidelines for large sidecars.

The sidecar's wheel lead of 11 inches was measured along the longitudinal, from the hub of the motorcycle's rear wheel to the hub of the sidecar's wheel. It was also within suggested guidelines and, again, it could not have been changed without major welding operations.

Then I pushed the front of the sidecar a tiny little bit inward toward the front wheel of the motorcycle, achieving the recom-mended sidecar *toe-in* of ¾ inch (see Figure on the left). This toe-in has the same function as the toe-in of the front wheels of a car, namely, to affect a car's propensity to roll forward in a straight line. Now, I reconnected all adjustable connecting rods and fixed the rod settings and with them, the positioning of the sidecar in reference to the motorcycle.

Finally, I measured the sidecar's levels. The sidecar leaned 3° forward, nose down toward the front of the rig. It also leaned 1° toward the right, away from the motorcycle, called lean-out. The two angles, I learned from the literature, do not affect driving parameters much, but the sidecar' lean-out may change the wear pattern of the sidecar tire. I could not adjust it anyway since the sidecar's attachment points to the motorcycle's sub-frame fixed the height of the sidecar on its left (motorcycle side). On its right (opposite side) the sidecar wheel and tire sizes determined the height of the sidecar on the right side and thus its leaning angle.

There were no adjustments at the wheel mount to the sidecar, which could have raised or lowered the wheel with reference to the sidecar. With the fixed attachment point to the motorcycle, the lean-out of the sidecar was therefore only adjustable by the sidecar's rim and/or tire size. A larger tire would have raised the sidecar and thus adjusted the leaning angle. That very fact may have been the real reason why my predecessor had installed the larger Wal-Mart tire. Since the little lean is not considered to affect driving properties I felt safe with a smaller motorcycle tire that I had bought for the sidecar. The smaller tire also increased its distance from the fender attachment rod mentioned earlier.

To assure the motorcycle's lean-out angle I re-measured it several times during the entire set- up process and I confirmed its accuracy with a large, 3 foot carpenter's right angle. Then I test-drove the motorcycle several times on city streets and highways. The driving and steering feel were now excellent: at a steady speed the motorcycle maintained a straight forward direction, pulling only a little to the right when I increased speed, or to the left when I reduced the speed – just as it should be for a well tuned rig. The motorcycle responded easily to my slightest steering attempts telling me that the track width was just right for the weight and size of the rig. During all of this tuning, I also learned that the parameters would be different for an empty or a fully occupied sidecar. Since I mostly drove alone, I set all the parameters for an unoccupied sidecar knowing that a fully loaded sidecar would have a greater tendency to pull to the right.

Tuning the rig attachment seemed to have been most successful since my back pain seized to my great surprise. Do you now understand how rewarding it can be, to tinker with your own motorcycle?

Test Drive Between The Two Rivers

Then, on the first summer-like day in April it was time to evaluate the rig's long-distance performance. After a very stormy night, with tornado warnings for the north of Columbus toward the town of Delaware and further northeast areas, I was curious to see what kind of storm damage was to be seen and used this as a good reason for the drive. I rode along the gorgeous Olentangy river north to Delaware. There I turned west onto SR 42. When I reached the Scioto River, I turned onto SR 256 south along that scenic river. Finally, I turned east on Home Road, met Olentangy River Road again (Ohio 315), and followed it south toward home. It took exactly 60 minutes for a 50 miles stretch. Bright sun with large white clouds, chasing on a light blue sky, made this trip a beautiful experience. The fields were coated in a fresh light green and the gardens were at their spring blooming peak. Very little traffic shared the roads with me, and the motorcycle ran smoothly, humming quietly along the road and gobbling up the miles. The steering was soft and very direct with greatly diminished drag toward either side, making the ride comfortable for the entire hour. The greater tire inflation (now 40 psi in all three new tires) may have added to the lighter steering feel.

An occasional strong crosswind, however, affected the steering noticeably pushing the rig sideward. A solo motorcycle would naturally lean against the blowing wind, but with my rig, I had to hold the steering against the wind and it required my full attention to maintain the proper driving direction. This was, I believe, not a problem of proper linkage but rather an inherent challenge of the engineering limitations of a rig. The rig was now in its best-tuned condition since I bought it in 2006, and I was overjoyed.

My only remaining disappointment with the rig's performance was its fuel consumption. Originally, low fuel consumption had been my "justification" for owning a motorcycle. Yet, this rig averaged only 27-28 mpg of super (94 octane) gasoline. Although this was better than almost all cars on the market of those days, it did not even come close to the consumption of Gudrun's new Toyota Prius, which averaged 50 miles per gallon of *normal* (89 octane) gasoline. Unfortunately, there was little that could be done about it since the sidecar added a significant overall drag to the

53

motorcycle resulting in the higher gasoline consumption. Furthermore the engine was built in 1984 and had run at least 75 thousand miles according to the defective odometer. Possibly, its cylinders and pistons could be reworked to improve performance, but I could not justify re-building the engine, which might have costed me a good $3,000.

Up to Cleveland

For quite some time, I had hoped to take a longer trip over night to visit my children in Cleveland Heights: Horst and Erin. Jonathan had offered to join me on his motorcycle, but it took some diligent planning to nail down a time when we were both free, when the weather was dry and not too warm, when our wives were positively inclined to allow or even partake in this trip, and when the date suited our children in Cleveland Heights. And then, one day, Jonathan had to use up his last vacation day, and when Elsa was suddenly out of a job. So, we set Friday August 22 as a target date and then everything fell into place. The weather turned out to be perfect. A thin layer of clouds covered the sky and there was no rain forecasted. The temperature around 82° F was pleasant for biking. We left Thursday afternoon at 4 pm. The tour toward Cleveland was to be quick, so that we could arrive there at or before 9 pm. We took SR 3 northeast to Wooster. There, we had a dinner sandwich at the side of the road, and then we turned onto SR 585, which continued in the same NE direction. Near Norton/Barberton we turned north onto SR 21, which brought us onto Cleveland's outer ring, US 271. We followed it east until the Cedar Road exit, which brought us to Cleveland Heights. There we arrived at 9 pm, sharply.

Besides my Children Horst & Erin, my nephew Johannes von Recum was there also. He was visiting his cousins Horst and Erin and to work in Horst's research lab for a prolonged summer. Together we went into town to eat an ice cream. Next morning, after a scone breakfast, we left at 8 am to return home. We passed Norton again but then stayed on SR 21 continuing southward until Massillon with the intent to take SR 62 back home. The last road stretch of SR 21, however, starting at Norton and ending north of Massillon was in poor road surface condition, which made the ride for pregnant Elsa in the sidecar quite uncomfortable. This poor road quality was, in our experience with Ohio's roads very unusual. So, we turned onto a very small CR 44 and traveled it south, right through beautiful Amish farming communities and scenic farmland, until we reached SR 62/37, which took us west for a few miles into Millersburg.

In Millersburg, we parked our motorcycles next to the courthouse. We took a picture of the horse buggy of a courthouse visitor and had lunch in a comfortable, little, downtown hotel and restaurant, which reminded me of Germany's hotel culture of the late fifties. Refreshed and relaxed, we rode home following SR 62. The most beautiful part of the trip was up and down the little stretch of CR 44 through Holms County.

An Amish Buggy, Courthouse in Millersburg, 2008.

In the above shown photo of the Millersburg Courthouse, one can see a predecessor of my rig, an Amish horse-and-buggy team. Its driver may have had to take care of some legal business in the courthouse while the horse waited patiently and tolerated our touristic curiosity. To me, the buggy was a feast of esthetics. In spite of its square body and tall wheels it conveyed lightness, surely designed to conserve "horse-power" rather than convey earthly beauty or comfort.

That day we had traveled 207 miles, the previous day 163 miles, altogether 370 miles in perfect weather and riding conditions. Motorcycles and riders passed the endurance test with *magna cum laude*. Gasoline consumption for my rig was again 27 miles/gallon. The steering of the rig was good. There was no rattling or excessive vibration. Our average speed was 60 miles/hr. read on my speedometer, which compared to 55 miles/hr. on Jonathan's speedometer. Normally, that same trip to Cleveland using the I-71/271 takes 2.5 hours by car traveling 70 miles per hour, whereas the trip on secondary roads took us obviously double the time.

The Hack'd Re-Union Rally

By now the rig and I were mechanically and mentally ready for a long trip to Buckhannon in West Virginia. Hidden in the hills there was a Hack'd (colloquialism for rig) re-union rally on October 3 and 4. Jonathan and I left for the sidecar meeting Friday morning at 9:30 AM. Google calculated 234 miles (one way) for the trip. We arrived there at 5 PM. Rigs from all over the US gathered on the private property of the host, Jim Dodson. The property lay about three miles off SR 20 towards east and up the hill country at a hillside in the Teter area, near Hodgesville, West Virginia. The site was many acres large and was kept up well like an English park or a well cared for American campground: it was picked clean and freshly mowed. There were portable toilets and a shower facility. Jim Dodson was the editor of Hack'd, a magazine for and about sidecar enthusiasts. He had started rigging rigs (hacks) on order after his retirement seven years ago.

Jonathan and I had planned to get there taking SR 33 south from Columbus to Athens, then turning onto SR 50 east to Clarksburg WV. From there, we traveled SR 20 south to Hodgesville. In that little town we happened to meet another rig driver who knew the rest of the way up the winding back roads to the meeting place in the hills. He had come from Mexico City with his wife who only spoke Spanish while he said he was a North American, English speaking, retired Jew. Throughout the entire ride we experienced beautiful weather and 65° F which turned out to be the most pleasant driving temperature. Every two hours we had stopped to stretch our legs and drink something stimulating. At noon, we had eaten and refilled our gasoline tanks. SR 33 and 50 were predominately four-lane highways. They allowed for speedy travel but gave little scenic sightseeing opportunity. SR 20 in West Virginia, however, was a small local road and we enjoyed a more interesting travel through rugged landscapes, worthy of the good name West Virginia has among motorcyclists.

At our destination, a few grey haired older men in faded blue overalls, probably also rig drivers, stood around, waiting for things to happen. Sporting long grey beards and a reserved demeanor they spun local small talk with each other. In the center of the property, in an open shed, coffee, tea, chocolate drinks, and cake were offered for the self-help. Over the rest of the late afternoon and evening, more guests dribbled in slowly, almost all of them drove rigs. Our host, it was said, had built most of those rigs (which was the reason for the annual meeting's named "Re-Union"). Characteristic for this meeting appeared to be the assembly of un-characteristic rigs, each one a unique combination of old and new motorcycles and chairs. There were no two rigs alike. I saw four BMW K100 with various sidecars, two, more recent BMW models (one may have been a K1200, another one a R1150), and four URAL rigs. The URAL rigs are reproductions of the German 1937 BMW R71 rigs, manufactured in Russia since 1941, and marketed with recent, only minor alterations still today. There were also two or three Honda Goldwings, and about the same number of Harley-Davidsons. Their various chairs ranged from the smallest, torpedo-shaped body that might barely be comfortable for a slender teenager to a mini car-like chamber accommodating two full size passengers sitting next to each other with ease. All of them were in good appearance and shined up for this weekend event.

On the grounds, we met the latter Greg, the former owner of my rig, and later, we met the former Greg who had actually built the rig. We enjoyed each other in this unexpected re-union around my rig and naturally, we had some conversation about it. The former Greg came on a Honda Goldwing with a big, luxurious sidecar, which was occupied by his wife. The latter Greg came on a solo motorcycle, I believe a Suzuki. He said, that his K100 with sidecar was not ready to drive yet. In the picture below, Jonathan hat just finished setting up our tent in the back and our motor-

57

cycles were parked in front and the latter Greg had come for a chat. I had hoped to get some advice from either Greg on the engine noises that I was sure I heard emanating from my motorcycle's drive train.

Greg TenBrook visiting our camp, 2008.

They listened willingly and attentively to the engine and claimed not to hear anything abnormal, even though both had extensive experience with K100s. They felt comfortable with my noises but perhaps not with my question. Then, again, I might have had to accept that older engines do have looser bearings and cylinders and consequently noisier engines. I think, my question really was, how much engine noise reflects acceptable aging, and when does it start to be pathologic and crying for repair. To my disappointment and perhaps naiveté, there was no diagnostic help coming from them and so we turned to talking about the weather and the beautiful place at which we were meeting.

At about 6 PM, there was an evening meal. Dishes with cooked white rice, warmed cheese noodles, cooked potatoes, and hot, re-fried beans were placed on a long church picnic table. Bread and sausages were served out of their plastic bags; the attendees heated their hot dogs over a large open fire a few yards away from the tables. A dozen of green sticks had been cut and kindly placed next to the fireplace for that purpose. All sorts of soft drinks were available except alcohol. Nobody drank alcohol – amazing! After sundown, the people congregated around the open fire, around the dinner serving table, or in smaller groups else-where around rigs. When the mosquitoes became a bother to us around 7 PM, Jonathan and I retreated to our tent. At least I was tired and happy to go to sleep. The large campground had many nice and secluded tent sites; there may have been 20 tents and pop-up motorcycle trailers spread over a ten-acre meadow. By accident or design, the two Gregs and former owners of my motorcycle had their camp set up right in front of our site. Many other attendees may be fifty of them, stayed over night in close-by motels and joined us next morning when we prepared to take a joint trip. Altogether, a long train of rigs left at 8 AM to have a nice scenic drive for 3 hours, which ended at a local Lyons Club meeting place at the banks of a little creek.

For Jonathan and me it was an exciting experience to drive among about 50 or more rigs in a long line, through narrow mountain roads along a romantic mountain stream. The Lions clubhouse sat at the bank of the creek in the middle of the woods in fall colors. There, very friendly Lions Club members and their wives graciously served pancakes for $4 a person. The food was good and plentiful. Thereafter Jonathan and I returned to the campground, packed our stuff and left for home again, while many of the others seemed to have joined for another scenic trip in the later afternoon. My son-in-law Greg Broecker from Alexandria VA, who happened to travel with his motorcycle on the Virginia side of the mountains, saw the unusual sight of touring rigs and he phoned Gudrun to tell her about it.

For our trip back to Columbus, we picked a somewhat different tour to see more of the West Virginia mountain land-scape. The first part went along SR 20 north again to reach SR 50 at Clarksburg. From there, we took SR 50 toward west and the Ohio River. Shortly before reaching the Ohio River, we took SR 16 northwest until we came down to the river. There, at St. Mary's we ate lunch, crossed the river, and turned onto SR 7 north along the river. A little way north from St. Mary's a state park camping ground sat at the riverbanks. We stopped, walked shortly around that little park, and gazed at the giant and tranquil Ohio River.

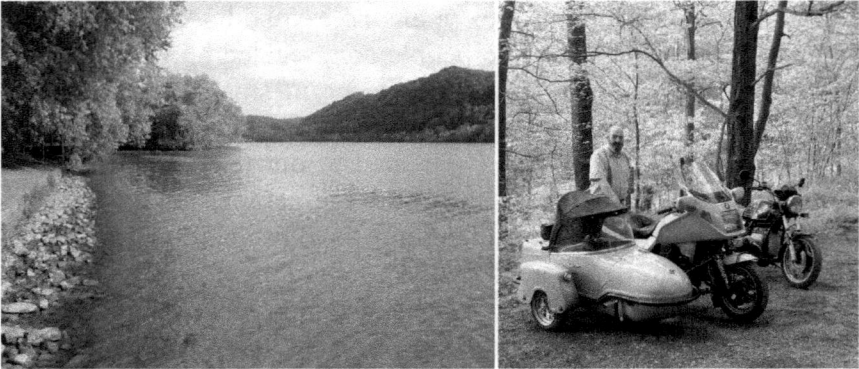

The Ohio River near St. Mary's, 2008 and Public Campground at the Ohio River (in the background), 2008.

We concluded, that this would be a nice place to go back to camp at another time[4]. Riding further north, we reached SR 800 and followed it northwest which brought us through beautiful and spacious hill country. When we reached US 70, we turned west on it for the last 115 miles toward home. That last stretch allowed us driving at a steady 70 miles per hour, but it still took two hours, which was exceedingly tiresome until we finally reached home around 6 PM. (On a long West Virginia bike trip in a subsequent year I learned to appreciate that, after a long day of exciting mountain roads, it was actually relaxing to drive the last part of the trip home on straight roads.)

After we had come down from the West Virginia hills to the altitude of the Ohio River, when we had reached the last stretch of our trip on the Interstate, and while we drove a continuous 70 miles/hour for 2 hours, a noise appeared to come from the front of my motorcycle. "Oh, no, not another noise," I thought, but this time it sounded softly like buffeting in the wind or like the hasted flapping (5/sec. frequency) of a loose part of the motorcycle or the sidecar, somewhere. It seemed to be related to speeds above 60 miles/hour as if an object was loose. I do not remember having heard that noise ever before but I also have never ridden the motorcycle at that speed for such a prolonged period. Although, I considered that some aspect of the frame or front fork or fairing was loose, I could not find any looseness. The noise seemed to

---

[4] Leith Run [OH], 44400 SR 7, New Matamoras OH 45767.

originate within the front of the motorcycle's fairing or engine block. Days later, I happened to read in the Motorcycle Vol.39 under Helmets, that *"at highway speeds, wind buffeting around your head creates a loud but low frequency noise, similar to bass speakers."* Is that what it was? This sensation may also be different with different helmets because I heard it with my full helmet but I could not reproduce that noise with my half helmet the next day.

Overall, however, this was a worthwhile trip. It convinced me again, that I had a good rig for traveling, not the most modern, not too fancy, not the most comfortable as compared to some rigs we saw in West Virginia, but surely a stable, rugged motorcycle, with a well adjusted and comfortable sidecar at its side. I did not get backache anymore. My motorcycle, which was actually heavy and clumsy looking, turned out to be easily steered: a very comfortable long distance vehicle for the motorcycle enthusiast. Altogether, we drove 530 miles over that weekend. My motorcycle consumed a total of 19 gallons of high-octane (93) gasoline, averaging 27.89 miles per gallon and costing me $70 or one dollar for every 7.6 miles.

Were There Transmission Problems?

By now, the reader might have detected my hypersensitivity, when it comes to noises. I was always weary of unusual noises and searched for their possible origins. I was always afraid that these noises might be early indicators of something major going wrong and compromising the safety of my ride. Unfortunately, I knew nothing about the power train's mechanical history, not even its actually accrued mileage.

To my hearing, three different types of noises came from my power train. A high pitch pinging or tingling at lower rpm appeared especially when the engine was still cold. It seemed to me that this noise related to ignition timing or perhaps to piston slap. Then there was a metallic rattling which was best heard at the front and left side of the power train, predominately, again, during the first 5 to 10 miles of driving when the engine was still cold. It seemed not to be regular such as within the rhythm of the valve or piston motion. Judged from the web literature a loose, or insufficiently lubricated cam chain came to my mind. The third noise appeared during the same warm-up period, but was a low pitch, hard *"knokkkking"*, best heard on the right (sidecar) side of the power train, and it seemed to be rhythmical, related to main shaft rotations. Did it point to a loose rod or bearing within the power train?

My first preventative actions were to put the motorcycle on a high-octane diet, exclusively. Although the previous owner had instructed me, that the K100 would thrive on low octane rated gasoline, my decision proved right and the pinging noise coming from the cold engine at low rpm disappeared. Then I changed engine and transmission oil brands to full synthetic ones to use those ever since. Doing so, I felt a little like a physician or veterinarian who may administer a shot of antibiotic and/or cortisone as a first measure of precaution, until the real source of illness is diagnosed and targeted with a more specific treatment regimen. My decisions seemed to be good ones for the time being and the noises dimmed down somewhat for a while.

Although the BMW expert at Honda Northwest said he could not hear the noises, but he suggested replacing the cam chain and tensioner at the time of the next routine 10K service. He added, that for him to be able to do that, I would have to remove the sidecar and sub-frame first. This then was the time for me to learn to disconnect the sidecar. Luckily, my son-in-law Greg was visiting at that time and he disconnected the sidecar with the help of his 10 year old son Stefan, while the rest of the family (including me) attended the wedding of my youngest daughter Elsa. A day later, three of my sons and a kind neighbor loaded the solo motorcycle without fairing and headlight, onto the neighbor's utility trailer and we hauled it to the shop. When I had the motorcycle back, I spent a week to re-connect the sidecar. The total cost of this repair session was a whopping $1,600. After this work-intensive, and expensive repair, there were still some of the noises left especially when the engine was cold. Did I get good advice? Had I made the right decisions?

Some time later, when I attended the General Assembly of the Orthodox Presbyterian Church in Michigan, I met a delegate, may be in his mid-thirties, who told me that he had been repairing Harley-Davidson motorcycles for a living during the past 15 years. "By your looks," he said to me with a kind smile, "you ride a

BMW". I was fascinated by his guess and confirmed that I was, but that I was always hearing things in the power train and that I was always worried that something might soon be going very wrong. He still smiled and said, "you should not be worried because you own the best of the best". He continued saying that "motorcycle owners often come and claim that they are hearing things. It would be too expensive to open up the power train merely on the suspicion that something might be wrong," he said, "I always recommended that the motorcycle owner come back when something had actually gone wrong." "But you do not need to worry", he repeated, saying, "You have a BMW". He was so kind!

One year later, during the previously described West Virginia sidecar weekend, I met both previous owners of the rig. As I had already described earlier, I had them listen to the engine and they claimed they did not hear unusual noises. I did not further interrogate them as to what they meant by "unusual", but when I came home from that very trip there was a heavy leak of transmission oil from the pressure relief valve of the final drive. In fact, oil had spewed all over the rear end of the motorcycle: the wheel, the tire, and the disk break; all had a freshly oiled shine about them like the bodies of bodybuilders. When I drained the oil from the final drive, it had a dirty, creamy, light brownish, foamy, turbid appearance. Surprisingly, within a few miles driving, the oil pressure built up again in the final drive. After I had drained the final drive three times within a week, I consulted again my BMW expert and he diagnosed that the oil gain in the final drive stemmed from a leak along the splines from the transmission. From the drained oil, he also diagnosed heavy wear within the transmission and the final drive.

Again, in order to get this repair done I had to remove the chair and bring the solo motorcycle to the BMW service, and so I disconnected the sidecar again. By now, I had learned to disconnect the sidecar myself within a short two hours. Then Jonathan drove the solo motorcycle to the shop. One month and $2,000 later, I picked up the repaired and serviced motorcycle with my own utility trailer. It took me two solid 8-hour days to re-attach the sidecar and the fairing. The benefit of this re-attachment was that by now I knew how to do it well and avoid the many little mistakes I had committed in earlier times. Purchasing the transmission and the final drive was another $1,000 decision even though I obtained used parts from Re-Psychle, an excellent BMW used-parts dealer in Lithopolis OH. Again, a mayor 10k miles service was combined with this repair, and the front tire was replaced adding up to a total labor bill of $1,600. If some of the noises I had heard all along, had originated within the transmission, they should be gone now!

On January 2, 2009, I did the first test drive and rode about 10 miles on highways and city streets. The motorcycle ran smoothly and responded much better to throttle changes than it ever did before. The gear shifted easier and more reliable. The engine rattle was gone but instead I heard a healthy, deep, humming related to the speed of driving and not to the engine's rpm. Some of that newly heard humming might have related to the three new tires on the rig, but whatever the source of origin was, it sounded comfortable. Driving now with this new-old transmission and without undue noises or oil leaks gave me a wonderful sense of safety.

The sidecar followed the motorcycle well. The steering was even easier and more responsive then before, possibly relating to the round profile of the new tires and the good setting parameters of the sidecar linkage. Now I knew how a running K100 should sound and how a rig should drive. Now it felt like riding a sensitive Lipizzaner stallion that responds powerfully to the slightest cues of the rider -- rather than sitting on a slow draft horse that is full of power but has little sensitivity to the rider's cues. This was, how I had always fancied a BMW motorcycle would perform. Now it did.

For the following pages I have selected a few motorcycle trips that had special meaning to me, because they taught me about Ohio's landscape and culture. They also helped develop a close friendship with my youngest son-in-law, Jonathan Meyer. Many other trips were recorded in the archives of my life but did not make it into this document.

The Beauty of Southeastern Ohio

Besides all the motorcycle repairs, there was ample time to tour the State of Ohio and to discover attractive landscapes and cities in the State. From the few trips I had already taken into various directions of Ohio I concluded that from a biking point of view, the regions south, southeast, and east of Columbus are the most exciting ones. They coincide with the foothills of the Appalachian Mountains. Their landscape of gentle hills, rocky hollows, and valleys provide a variety of scenery that appeals to the eye and to the imagination of a city dweller like me. That area is officially divided into Southern Ohio, Southeast Ohio, and East Central Ohio, and most of my travels on motorcycle have focused on those areas.

The little Morgan County seat, the village of McConnelsville impressed me most with its charm. Driving south from I-70, along SR 60, which follows the east bank of the Muskingum River, McConnelsville sits on top of a small hill above the river, which was once an important shipping route. Wedged in between the hills and the river valley it used to benefit from its strategic location at the river. Now the town represents the hub for Morgan County road traffic. On the west side of the river, State Routes 78 and 377 combine with 37 and cross the river jointly. In town, on the east side of the river, they meet Routes 60, and 376 only to split up again, each following its own direction. The town now accommodates about 17 hundred citizens.

Downtown McConnelsville (Tim Kiser, Wikimedia Commons)

The town's center square is actually diamond shaped and allows the crossing of Ohio Routes 60, 78, and 376. A life-size civil war soldier in bronze represents the center point of the square and may be even of the town. An impressive-sized, two-part commercial/residential building block dominates the square, sitting in one of its corners. Built during the Victorian period its red brick façade is styled in modest Richardsonian Romanesque arrangements and gives the impression of a small courthouse or town hall.

I had passed through that town a number of times, first when alone I scouted the beautiful southeast of the state, then another time when Jonathan and I spent a Friday circling around Hocking Hills. Both times McConnelsville was not actually the goal of our trips and, still, we discovered its charm while passing through. Its rural county seat activities and pride of the local history captured my fascination every time, perhaps because it reminded me of the county seat in Germany where I grew up. Then, later, my wife Gudrun and I visited McConnelsville in two successive years specifically to observe its special civil war reenactment. Gudrun had a general interest in reenactment of that period with its clothing and household items, the demonstration of war camps, and their carefully displayed simplicity in culture, technology, and discipline. The Historical Society of McConnelsville had adopted a very special detail of the civil war period, the Morgan's Raid, and the McConnelsville citizens annually celebrate its historical significance for their region:

It is said that John Hunt Morgan, a Confederate Brigadier General had come raiding through Morgan County. Coming from the west in July 1863, he crossed the Muskingum River at the Rokeby Lock, about 9 miles north of McConnelsville. Quickly, local militia formed to protect the county, and eventually accepted the surrender of General Morgan with 400 of his soldiers. The Historical Society of McConnelsville not only preserved this specific historical moment of their county, but also succeeded to rally the town and its people around a subject of common, local fate and pride. What made the re-enactment so special for Gudrun and me was that the "McConnelvillians" seemed to celebrate their past for their very own remembrance. The few out-of-town spectators we saw appeared to be there incidental. Beyond a few period traders offering items of the civil war epoch, there were no modern day booths selling mass-produced goodies or food and drinks, but there were more than a hundred citizens living and re-enacting in period, for them, a special day out of their very own venerated civil war past. On one hand, I wonder why there were so few tourists around to enjoy the tranquility of this charming tiny town, on the other hand that may be the very reason for the preservation of its own special character.

German Towns in East Central Ohio

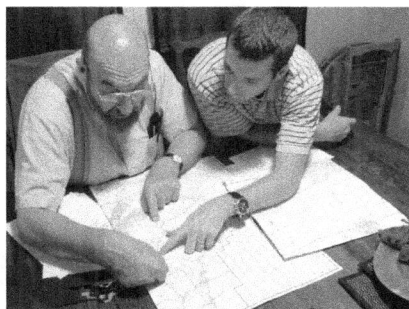

When they hear my German accent, many Ohioans tend to mention with considerable pride that German immigrants had played a leading role in the settlement and formation of Ohio, and they sometimes point to a few Ohio settlements with German names. Jonathan (right on picture), having German forefathers, also has expressed a special love for his country of origin. So we often talked about visiting some of these settlements to look for their German identity. Then, the time had come to become serious about it. It was the beginning of March, the last month of spring and early summer when mild weather of 60 to 70 degrees temperature could make such trips most enjoyable. Further considerations were that

Elsa expected her first baby sometime in June eliminating that month and later from our trip planning. Beyond that, the days in July, August, and the greater part of September, we surmised, would be too hot for relaxed, extended driving.

Jonathan had set the theme for this trip to be a visit to German settlements in Central/East Ohio. He picked four small villages located in a half circle around the east of Columbus including Berlin, Gnadenhutten, Dresden, and Bremen. For just incase, we dressed warmly with thermal underwear, layers of pullovers, pulse warmers, thick gloves, warm feelings, and great expectations. Because thick fog was announced for the next day, we started later in the morning than usual, hoping that the fog would have lifted by that time.

Berlin in Ohio's Holms County

On March 1, 2009 our first destination was Berlin in the Amish populated Holms County. While we traveled on the scenic US 62 toward northeast in mid-morning, we still experienced thick fog starting at Danville. Its moisture settled on our clothes as millions of little water bubbles. The air temperature around 32°F made this the longest stretch of road to bear: It was so cold!

Ready to leave (G. von RECUM, 2009).

After two hours driving and shivering, we stopped at a fast food place outside of Millersburg. A hot drink warmed us up a little and helped to overcome our nagging feeling that this trip might have been a bad idea, but since there was only 10 more miles toward Berlin we continued the trip. By the time we had arrived there, the sun had just come out and dispersed the fog. So, we walked around that busy little tourist town on the hilltop and to warm up in the newly warming sunshine.

The town of Berlin is reported to be the oldest existing village in Holmes County, having been drawn-up on July 2, 1816. A man by the name of John Swigert, a supposed native from Berlin, Germany (with apparently Anglicized name) arranged for 108 lots to be laid out along an east and west street and a north and south street. Mr. Swigert and another early settler, Joseph Troyer from Berlin, Pennsylvania named the town after their respective hometowns. Folklore suggests that Swigert chose the site of Berlin because its elevation, the highest in Holmes County, made its defense more feasible in case of an attack by Indians.

During the 19th century, there was much industry in Berlin. It boasted of machine shops, a foundry, dry goods stores, hotels, tailor shops, hat factories, blacksmith shops, a tannery, and a gristmill. A hugely successful Berlin farmers auctions had been moved out of town a little bit up north to Mt. Hope where there was enough open space for the auction and for parking.

A school and a post office were started in 1818. A number of churches were a part of early Berlin history including Methodist, Presbyterian, Baptist, and Mennonite. Amish settlers did not come into Berlin Township in any significant numbers before 1820. Most of the early settlers of the Berlin area originated from Germany and Switzerland, first settling in Pennsylvania, then migrating to Ohio. The first Amish congregation in this area was established around 1820. Today, Berlin is considered the center of the world's largest Amish settlement. The Amish means of transport was the same then as it is today, horse drawn carriages and wagons.

Even though it had been a chilling cold morning, the sun had come up, the sky was light blue and we both started to warm up. Berlin is a very small town with supposedly 530 citizens. It serves as a regional shopping center to the Amish people who buy sewing supplies, hardware, harness, and buggy supplies. There they also sell their own products such as fruit and vegetables, baked goods, milk, cheese, candies, woodcrafts, furniture, baskets, and supplies for sewing crafts. In addition the Amish catered to the newest fashion of selling mixed-breed toy puppies in large quantities to the "English". Because of this aggregation of Amish people and their products, Berlin has also become a year-round tourist attraction. Beyond the Amish products, there are now kitschy craft stores selling the same stuff you can buy at any other tourist trap in the nation, such as at the Grand Canyon, Hawaii, or Dodge City. Busloads of tourists roam the tiny little village, buy goodies, and gaze at "the plain people", while the local Amish do their own trading or service in some of these stores and restaurants, but stay humbly and reverend in the background in spite of the great attraction they represent to the visitors.

Because Berlin occupies the junction of US Route 62 and SR 39, cars and heavy trucks crawl in a continuous line up the steep incline of Main Street all day long. We wondered why the through fair traffic was not led around the town to allow for a quieter town and less noisy sightseeing.

Our walk through town had raised our comfort and the good smell of the exhibited pastries made us hungry but we decided to have lunch at a quieter place. We chose Guggisberg a few miles east of Berlin. Built, as another tourist attraction there was a restaurant and a cheese factory, open for visitors to observe how cheese is made in Ohio's Amish country. The buildings resembled Swiss Alpine style, whereas the cheese and the food in the restaurant seemed to be a mixture of supposedly Swiss cooking and Amish plainness to fit the average American consumer tastes best. The servers were dressed in Swiss dirndls and wore a jolly, green national-dress-hat with a white feather. The friendly young girl, who served us, tried some German phrases on us and we responded in German. Then we continued our trip further eastward to Gnadenhutten.

Gnadenhutten in Ohio's Tuscarawas County

The original German word Gnadenhutten was most likely spelled with the umlaut *ü, "Gnadenhütten"*. This village was tugged away on SR 36 near New Philadelphia but was a remarkably clean and well laid-out village, located in south central Tuscarawas County. According to the 2002 census it had a population of about 1,300. It spread out in a valley partly surrounded by hills, with the Tuscarawas River flowing along its southwest border.

Recorded history tells us, that in 1772, a Moravian missionary Rev. David Zeisberger founded Gnadenhutten ("Huts of Grace" would be a good translation from German). The American Revolution, however, made life difficult for the residents of Gnadenhutten and other nearby Moravian settlements. During the war, non-Christian Delaware Indians supported England instead of the rebellious Americans but the Christian Indians hoped to remain neutral. In March 1782, American revolutionaries in retaliation for raids falsely attacked the village, captured the inhabitants, and murdered 96 of them. This gruesome event became known as the Gnadenhutten Massacre. The Moravians never rebuilt the village after the incident, meaning that today's buildings have nothing in common with the time of the massacre except their fit into the original town plan.

We parked our motorcycles at the edge of the village and walked through today's small settlement. The two principal streets, Walnut and Main met perpendicular in the middle of the town. They did not resemble the classical downtown business area but were lined with residential homes and gardens. The houses were small, built in the style of the 19th century and onward, and were kept up neatly. We were impressed by an obvious concern for a clean, orderly, and beautiful, suburban like appearance.

When we filled our gas tanks at the junction of Walnut and Main, I asked the gas station attendant where the town's shopping centers were, and she said that we would have to drive 17 miles further east or 30 miles west to do our shopping. May be this was the reason why this village looked so clean and functional – there was no shopping malls killing the local business and livelihood of small American towns. With full gasoline tanks, we then headed south toward Coshocton to see our next goal, Dresden.

Dresden in Ohio's Muskingum County

Near the former site of the Delaware Indian village of Wakatomika we found the village of Dresden, next to the Wakatomika Creek that drains into the Muskingum River near the northern edge of the village. The Indian settlement was burned down in 1794 during Lord Dunmore's War, opening the area for White settlement. I could not find any information on who started the white settlement and how the name of Dresden came about, but ancestries of today's citizens of Dresden, according to a recent census, were: German (25.4%), United States (16.2%), Irish (12.7%), English (8.4%), Dutch (1.8%), and Hungarian (1.8%). It was a hope for religious tolerance, though, that first brought large numbers of Germans and may be of other nationals to Dresden at a time when religious intolerance and unrest ruled in central Europe.

During the 19th century, Dresden was a trading settlement connected to the important transportation routes of the Ohio River and the Erie Canal. In 1825, the state legislature had authorized the construction of the Ohio Canal that would connect Lake Erie at Cleveland in the very north of the state with Portsmouth at the Ohio River in the very south of the State. A side canal at Dresden linked the Ohio and Erie Canal with the Muskingum River. After a short, booming business related to the canal, the advent of railways in the early1860s choked canal shipping but did not bring railway related business to Dresden.

Today, Dresden has a population of 1,423 according to the 2000 census. The village now has the feel of a bedroom community. There are very few signs of former wealth to be seen, except a large two or three story brick schoolhouse, which has been maintained but has not found a new main purpose for its continued existence. Most houses in the village were small, and in poor upkeep, underscoring the fact, that modern economy had deserted this village. At the turn to the twenties century, the Longaberger family (a name that could very well be of German origin) had started weaving baskets. Astoundingly, their business had grown into the largest basked manufacturing company of the North American Continent, employing about 40,000 people. Unfortunately for Dresden, it had moved out of the village years ago and re-located outside of Dresden nearer to Coshocton where there was more space for the factory layout and for customer parking. The

72

economical high days of this village were clearly in the past. A few stores in the center of Dresden catered to tourism with memorabilia and an artisanship of the past.

We passed by Prospect Place (also known as Trinway Mansion) just north of Dresden. This 29-room mansion was built in 1856 by abolitionist George Willison Adams. It is now listed on the National Register of Historic Places and on the Ohio Underground Railroad Association's list of Underground Railroad sites, and is used as the home of the not-for-profit G. W. Adams Educational Center, Inc.

Prospect Place, built 1856 (Web site).

Its simple-hipped roof, widely overhanging eaves, supported by decorative brackets, and a little, centered tower, are all hinting to the Italianate building style that dominated the early 19th century architecture.

Politically, Dresden played a role in the liberation of American slaves. From around 1812 to 1861 the Muskingum River, passing the village on its east side, was a major underground railroad route used by fugitives who escaped from the South on their journey north to Lake Erie and Canada.

Prospect Place featured many new and, for the time, revolutionary innovations. It had indoor plumbing, which included a copper tank cistern on the second floor, which pressurized water throughout the house. Two coal stoves had copper tanks (under pressure from the cistern system), which heated water and allowed the home to have both hot and cold running water service. This was the first house of the era in Muskingum County to have indoor flush toilets (water closets).

Because of the late hour we did not stop to visit the site but followed our urge to reach our next and final location, one American Bremen. In order to get to Bremen we took SR 60 further south, crossed under US 70, and passed through the middle of the city of Zanesville. By the time, we had reached the south end of Zanesville and because it was getting dark fast, we changed our plan, took some very small local routes back to US 70, and rushed home. There, Thomas, Katie, and Elsa waited with Gudrun to go out with us for a nice, warm dinner.

Bremen in Ohio's Fairfield County

Five weeks later, there was another opening in our calendars and the anticipation of a sunny day. Modern weather predicttions, as seen in television and in the daily newspapers have become so accurate, that we always relied on them for our tour planning. The prospect of good weather stimulated Jonathan and me to finish the goals of our previous trip to German towns.

Bremen, another small village with a German name, is located about one hour's drive southeast of Columbus. Its neighboring, larger town is Lancaster. George Berry is said to have founded Bremen in 1834 naming the new village after his father-in-law's hometown of Bremen in Germany. At first, the village grew slowly, functioning mainly as a service center for local farmers. In the 1850s, the railroad came to Bremen giving its economy a welcomed boost. By 1884, its population had increased to 200 inhabitants. Then in 1907, oil was discovered there. Due to the resulting boom, Bremen grew quickly, accumulated wealth, and developed local industry, some of which still seems to be in business today.

Bremen, according to the 2000 census, has a population of 1,265 but shows little of its past wealth. One company, dominating the center of the settlement still makes large oil drums and other supplies for the oil drilling industry, and at the north end of town, a large polymer producing company seems still to be in operation. One of the many oil derricks in town, originally built in the 1920s, had been relocated to the town's Howell Park and preserved there for sightseeing. In front of that derrick we found a horseshoe-throwing competition court with ten or more individual competition sites. Bremen, as it said on a billboard there, was National champion for a number of years in the past.

We drove back to downtown, as represented by the junction of Broad Street and Main Street, which may have been the only two streets of any importance. There was an old fashion restaurant and, because it was noontime we ate lunch there, Hamburgers and French fries were recommended to us. The restaurant was almost empty, except for a steadily growing cue of elderly people who were lining up inside the dining room along its outer wall. They obviously waited for some event. At first, we thought they might be assembling for a bus tour for senior citizens, perhaps visiting a casino somewhere else. When we had finished eating, and while we paid for our lunch, I asked one friendly man who stood there in line. "We are waiting for tickets for a music event featuring the fifties", he responded. The concert was to take place later that day in a back room of that same eatery. He felt sorry that we were not pre-registered and therefore would not get tickets for this event. He believed, however, that the band would play again at other times and that we might have a chance to get to hear the group then.

After lunch and because the day was still young, we continued our trip into the hilly country immediately southeast of Bremen. On the map, that area appeared like a large hill or forest without major roads leading into it. I learned later that the area was named Monday Creek Township of Perry County, where 671 people live today. This township surrounds the Little Monday Creek, a tributary to the Monday Creek of the Hocking River, which, in turn drains into the Ohio River. The land, first settled in the mid 18th century, was rich in natural resources such as iron ore, coal, salt, clay (for brick production), oil, and natural gas. Starting then, these resources were rigorously exploited, the land was deforested by 1885, and the water and the creek beds became severely polluted by acid mine drainage. As a result and according to Ohio Environmental Protection Agency (EPA) the Monday Creek was "irretrievably altered to the extent that no appreciable aquatic life can be supported."[5] This total exploitation of the land slowed down with a decline of the mined resources and eventually halted with the establishment of Wayne National Forest in 1935. A slow recovery of the land has taken place since then, with 87 percent secondary growth forest re-established, and local action further pursues restoration since 1994.

We circled around Monday Creek Township starting on CR 37 east to New Lexington. From there, we followed CR 93 which led us south and then west around that forest area until we reached Logan on SR 33. According to the report of the Monday Creek Restoration Project, there was no fishing possible and no recreation facilities, but we crossed over one or two marked hiking paths in support of some recreation activities. Most of the scenery now belongs to Wayne National Forest and looked like ideal for hunting raccoon and deer. Indeed, there were a number of road kills scattered along the road attesting to available game. We passed by small settlements including Bristol, McCuneville, Shanee, New Straitsville, Oreville, Gore, and Webb Summit. Some of those settlements had architectural reminders of a more profitable past and a bleak presence. There were closed down strip mines, empty ironworks, deserted brick factories, an abandoned movie theatre, and even newer manufacturing plants that seemed to have been closed only recently. Yet, the small residential homes that appeared along the road all along our trip looked well kept up. We saw well-attended garage sales where women stood in line to pay for their selected items. Many men were busy around their property, mowing lawns, chopping firewood, or working on equipment. The beautiful weather may have lured them out. In one yard there was a sign announcing the upcoming "Moonshine Festival", on another site, a spitting contest was advertised.

---

[5] The Institute for Local Government Administration and Rural Development at Ohio University; Rural Action, Inc. (January 1999). "A Comprehensive Plan for the Monday Creek Watershed: A Collaboration of The Partners of the Monday Creek Restoration Project and the Residents of the Monday Creek Watershed".

We drove exactly one hour from Bremen to Logan and it was an hour well spent on Ohio's rural history. It seems Ohio saw many great opportunities that developed for its people over the past two centuries, but then those vanished again. There were prolific sources of raw material to be tapped. There was low cost transportation such as the natural and manmade waterways and the later railways. All of these opportunities lured people into the area and brought work to many and wealth to some. Those rural people always had to adjust to drastic economical ups and downs. Settlements evolved and died. Waterways and later railways became booming sites for business and then lingered along. When they no longer supported their residents they were left to rot away.

And yet, we saw that at some houses along the road big rigs (tractor units for howling trailers and big equipment) were parked. They may have become the new life support for many in this remote area. Tractor-trailer units require good roads, which we observed here, and everywhere else in Ohio: The roads on all levels, US, State, and County were in excellent condition and care. Employment in transportation allowed people to maintain their residences in the hills and live there, while commuting to their work places in nearby cities or working on the road as drivers or road crews. With all the economic threats including exploitation of the land and pollution of its streams, I sensed that live was going on and new means of sustenance always seemed to develop to the flexible and able residents.

Summarizing the entire German Towns trip, we had spent 10 hours and traveled 250 miles through the East of central Ohio. After an initial bitter cold morning, we enjoyed the mild and sunny weather from lunchtime onward and we learned much about the rural past, and about our two motorcycles.

What is so German about Ohio's German Towns?

What I should have done before the trip was to study what exactly could be considered typically German in an American town that may be 200 years old or older? What characteristic goes as typical German, or when was what characteristically typical for German people, and who can make such generalizing judgments of **typical**?

According to the 2000 census, more than 40 million Americans out of a total resident population of 317,274,000,6 claimed German ancestry. Since the beginning of American colonization, Germans had a significant role in the development of American culture, economy, and religion, second only to the influence of the emigrants from the British islands. Furthermore, when we say German immigrants, it does not necessarily refer to people coming exclusively from a "State" of Germany. First of all the extent of the German state had varied considerably and often since the first time North America was settled in the 16th century. In addition, Central Europe accommodated many, very different German tribes with significantly different Germanic dialects and cultures including the Dutch, Swiss, and Austrian. Furthermore, their different ethnic neighbors such as the French in the West, the Slaves in the East, the Scandinavians in the North, and the Italians in the South, all had major linguistic, cultural, and political influence on their respective German neighbor.

In addition, many German-speaking immigrants came from European regions that were non-Germanic Nations, where they had lived as ethnic minority. I am thinking of examples like Alsace, Hungary, Rumania, Russia, Moravia, Poland, East Prussia and the Baltic countries. If all of those people were typically German, then what characteristics were so "typical" about them or their settlements?

A third difficulty in making generalized characterizations is the perspective (or bias) of the person who makes such a judgment. The German people, as far as I have experienced in my life, have (or used to have) very different socio-economical classes, which were distinctive culturally, economically, educationnally, and religiously definable. They evolved over the German history based on different tribal backgrounds and later religious forces. Can they all fall under some unifying character-ristics?

In my experience, people of the former class of the German nobility for example represented a broader, more western European behavior, while artisans and farmers were characterized by more narrowly definable and specific geographical regions. There is good scientific evidence published by David Hackett Fischer[6] that societal characteristics of four different immigrant groups out of the England of two hundred and more years ago, formed societal characteristics of regions in the New World, some of them continue to last into our times of today. Fischer's argument is that the culture of each of the studied groups from the British Islands was decidedly different but persisted, and that these cultures each provided some basis for the modern United States.

Lastly, the various cultures in Germany have changed with time, just like those in North America; so, when we talk about something typical German we have to state first what German period are we considering.

What really united German-speaking people since the 16th century was, in my mind, the creation of the High German language and some educational outcomes such as a love for system and order in education and perfection in workmanship, science, art, music, medicine, and philosophy? Furthermore, German people were raised to believe in the wellbeing of their society, and to respect and submit to authority of any kind. Finally, they were raised to adhere to their religious culture (either Roman Catho-licism or Protestantism). Some of all of this might still be true for the Germans in the Germany of today, but none of these can readily be discerned when one drives casually through the American countryside. There are at least two great exceptions in my limited experience, and those are the Amish lifestyle of the 18th century southwestern, Alemannic Germany which persists almost unchanged in the US, and German Village in downtown Columbus. Its layout, the architecture and building materials of its houses, and their little, fenced-in front and backyard gardens remind me and others of German middleclass sensibilities of the Biedermeier (Neoclassical) period of the mid 19th century with its simplicity, mobility and functionality. We could find none of that

---

[6] David Hackett Fischer, Albion's Seed, Oxford University Press, 1989, p. 6.

in our visited villages with German names. As we learned later, there were actually political advantages during the early 20th century to abandon purposefully promoted German appearances.

German immigration into Ohio boomed during the 19th century. By 1830, it had increased more than tenfold. Many towns in central Ohio were established in the first quarter of the 19th century. By 1832, more than 10,000 immigrants arrived from Germany in the US. By 1854, that number had jumped to nearly 200,000 immigrants.

There were many different reasons for the German influx: Many individuals left their fatherland because of the Germanic inheritance laws of primogeniture, giving the inheritance only to the oldest son and none to girls or the other male siblings; they had to build their existence elsewhere. Furthermore, entire religious groups came seeking freedom from suppression or persecution by the established state religions (Lutheran Protestantism, the Reformed [Calvinistic] Church, or Roman Catholicism). Thirdly, a large number of middle class people came during the mid 19th century, especially to Ohio because their hopes for a budding democratic government in Germany had been crushed by the actions of Duke Otto von Bismarck who as the chancellor of the Kingdom of Prussia, established a new, autocratic, united German empire. After the German Revolution of the middle class of 1848 failed, prospects in the United States seemed bright. For many it appeared easier to leave Germany and build a new existence from scrap in a new land that offered religious and political freedom.

German immigrants exerted great influence on many aspects of the cultural evolution of North America in such fields as agriculture, forestry, medicine, philosophy, theology, psychology, commerce, transportation, arts and sciences, architecture, printing, and education. Then, however, the outbreak of WWI drastically curtailed that German influence. Anti-German sentiments of the public and even of the government suppressed the speaking and teaching of the German language and culture. Many German names of people, businesses, and places suddenly disappeared. The anti-German sentiment continued through WWII and the immediate postwar years. Many German settlements and towns lost their German identity, even though some of their names remained German.

This was what we concluded from traveling through the towns with German names: Although they may have been founded and settled by German speaking people, Germanic characteristics, if there had been any, became homogenized within the melting pot of an all-absorbing American way of life. This was even true for the Amish occupied town of Berlin. Although the Amish people consciously and actively work to maintain strict separation from the American (English) culture around them, American economy has still invaded that town thoroughly, making the Amish way of life the very focus and museum's object of a highly comercialized tourism.

Jonathan and I concluded that a German influence could no longer be discerned in the outward appearance of these four towns. But we also concluded that a great many Ohioans are proud of their German forefathers and their influence on the culture, and government of this beautiful state of Ohio.

Camping Near Marietta in Washington County

Since our motorcycles were in good running order, since Elsa and Gudrun were planning to attend baby showers over the weekend of May 9 and 10, since Jonathan had work-free days of Thursday and Friday that week, and because I was available and eager to drive at any time, all the signs seemed set right for that weekend. We planned to leave Thursday May 7 early in the Morning and return Saturday May 9 sometime late afternoon. Elsa and Gudrun were agreeable with this trip and its timeframe pending good weather. During the prior week, the weather was nice and warm and we looked forward to an agreeable weather report. Unfortunately, with Thursday approaching the weather predictions on television were disappointing. Wednesday evening weekend temperatures were predicted in the low sixties, and thunderstorms were expected 50 percent of the time throughout Ohio's Southeast for the entire weekend. What was to be done?

Having spent so much time and effort in coordinating our calendars, achieving consent for the trip, and packing the motorcycles, we decided to wing it and see how far we would get before we would drown in rain.

We had packed a tent, air mattresses, sleeping bags, extra clothing, cooking utensils, and food for three days. My sidecar became the packhorse. When we left Thursday morning at 9 o'clock, the weather was just right for motorcycle riding: overcast skies without rain, temperatures between 65 and 78°F, minimal winds, and occasional clear skies with beautiful sunsets and sun rises surprised us throughout the following days. There was minimal traffic on the roads we traveled, and the road surfaces were excellent all the way, as we have become so accustomed to find in Ohio.

Since we could not communicate between the two riders while driving, we followed our preplanned routes through Southeast Ohio exactly. US 70 east brought us to Zanesville. From there, we followed SR 60 south to Marietta. From Zanesville until Marietta SR 60 follows the contours of the Muskingum River most of the time, which makes it a scenic route to follow. For a while, we rested at Lock 8 Rokeby, the last, hand-operated lock that still functions after two hundred years of operation. On the picture below, the presence of the lock can be guessed by the structure shown on the very left edge of the picture, and by the sudden current seen through the width of the river.

Rokeby, Lock 8 (left) at the Muskingum River (AvR, 2009).

In Marietta, we turned north onto SR 7, which follows the Ohio River on its west, the Ohio side. It brought us to the Leith Run Recreation Area a few miles north beyond Newport OH. We knew the place from a previous trip (to West Virginia) and we had planned to build our tent there as our base camp. From there then we had planned to spend the next day touring the adjacent hills of the Wayne National Forest, staying south of New Matamoras and SR 260, west of the Ohio River, north of Newport, and east of SR 26. Per telephone we had pre-arranged camping permission with the park management, as their website recommends.

When we arrived at the campground at 4 PM, it was closed. We halted our motorcycles at the closed entrance gate. Per cell phone, I asked the US Parks & Recreation Service in Marietta for advice. I did not even have to dismount my rig to get this help. A friendly ranger explained that the main water pipe of the campground had busted and flooded the campground. She suggested primitive camping for one night in the adjacent Wayne National Forest anywhere we wanted as long as we obeyed National Forest rules. Undoubtedly, cell phones had become a modern convenience even for the so-called "primitive" campers like us.

Immediately, we started to search for a suitable camping site along the west side of SR 7. We were looking for a dry and flat spot off the road, where we could park our motorcycles close by our tent. We rode along creeks that ran down from the wooded hills draining their water into the Ohio River. By 8 pm, we had found a place. It was off a graveled forestry road, on top of a ridge, and at the beginning of a foot trail called River Trail. By that time, the sky had cleared and the sun had just dipped below the horizon. Our choice spot appeared to be reasonably flat over an area of 12 x 12 feet and we pitched Jonathan's large family tent. Jonathan served as quartermaster, which also included the awesome responsibility for cocking.

Camping at the Edge of the River Trail (AvR, 2009).

As one can see from the picture above, a foot trail started right next to and to the left of our tent. Since there was a little time left before dark, we walked along the trail for some while and then, when the sun had left us to illuminate other parts of the world, we crawled into our sleeping bags to save us from the swarms of starving mosquitoes of that area.

The night was long and cold and the ground was not as flat and suitable for a comfortable rest as we had hoped. Around midnight a short burst of rain seemed to find a hole in the tent roof right above Jonathan's head. Raindrops hit first Jonathan and then the tent floor loudly and relentlessly. Since the tent was large enough for six to eight people, Jonathan could just roll over and away from the constant-drip cruelty of this State Forest. Eventually, I fell asleep in the early morning when the sun had not risen yet but when the first robins had started to sing and proclaim their rights for the upcoming day and potential robin brides.

We were definitely alone up there. As judged by barking housedogs, the next, closest residences, were more then half a mile away. The dogs' barking may have been their way to cope with the boredom of the night. They reminded me of a time when I stood in the South Carolina woods at night, listening what I thought was one of my hounds hunting a raccoon. When the barking appeared to become stationary. I stumbled through the thick and pitch dark under-wood to reach that site. When I came close enough to discern in the darkness which of my dogs it might have been, I found myself in the backyard of a house; a housedog sat there chained to an old, tossed over refrigerator that served him as his accommodation. He just barked there without apparent reasons, except, may be to communicate with some other chained-up dog elsewhere. My dogs where not found there. But let me come back to our campground.

The county gravel road on which we had arrived, I think it was called Number Nine, was about 50 feet away from our campsite. Throughout the night there were maybe two or three cars passing by us. At about 6 AM, one of those cars turned into our driveway. The driver looked at our tent and motorcycles from out of his car window, then turned his car around and left as quietly as a pickup truck can do. May be he or she was a ranger, or one of the neighbors who had heard us taking the evening before. I was so nicely rapped into my sleeping bag that I did not bother to get up and greet the visitor or at least check what he or she was doing, and, it seemed in hindsight, there was no need for it.

By 10 AM, we had collapsed our tent and packed it back into the sidecar, had eaten some breakfast that Jonathan had neatly prepared, and had left for a sight seeing trip through the hills of Wayne National Forest. Several county roads led up the hills along creeks and they were called by the creek's name such as Leigh Run, Sheets Run, Reas Run, or Davis Run. They had blacktop surfaces and wound up the hills inside steep and narrow ravines that were carved out of the mountain by the creeks' water. Somewhere on top of the hills, these county roads linked up with secondary county roads, which were also well maintained but graveled roads. They led along the top of ridges. Steep, wooded ledges often dropped off on both sides, but the view down the left or right side of the ridges was obstructed most of the time by dense forest that had just turned green with the new set of leaves. Few single houses stood among the trees along the gravel road or in little clearings. All morning, we saw only three men. They were working at their houses or their yards or on oil pumps next to the roads. Every house, it seemed, had a big dog tied up to a doghouse. Among them was a St. Bernard/Redbone mix (as the owner explained to me during a nice little chat), a Rhodesian ridgeback, a

Pyrenees Mountain Dog, and a very big German shepherd (as those three dogs were easily identified). They were impressively looking guards of those lonely properties and may very well be effective deterrents for strangers to intrude.

By noon, we reached Marietta. We did some sightseeing there, ate lunch in its historical Harmar Village, and strolled a little through Marietta's downtown. Marietta is claimed to be the oldest organized municipality in the state and the first official American settlement in the Northwest Territory for which reasons it became the government seat in 1788. Settled April 7, 1788 it benefited from its location at the junction of the Muskingum River and the Ohio River which once were important trade and transportation routes. Town buildings constructed from the late 18th century onwards and into modern days speak of a past rich civilization of trade. Bereft of its former trade and transportation dependent economy, it now struggles in keeping up a good façade for tourism. I felt a little ashamed that we were not spending more money there. This is still a very beautiful, little town embedded in a gentle, hilly landscape and encircled by the two major rivers. It would have been a nice place for my family and me to settle there in my retirement.

Just as in so many other American towns, not the church, but the courthouse occupied a central place in downtown and impressed us by its lavish, eclectic building style. I was fascinated by its stately appearance and so I started to collect a few pictures (see next page) of other state courthouses during my motorcycle travels. The courthouses shown there were built throughout the 19th century except the one in Marietta which was built, I believe, in 1901 in what I would call a Second Empire architectural style, popular in the late 19th century. Another such courthouse, which we saw during an earlier trip in New Lexington, is literally crowning the top of the hill in the middle of the town and it reaches far above all other buildings of that little town. Other representative courthouses out of the same architectural period we saw in Millersburg, Newark, Delaware (this one in a more modest Italianate style, reminiscent of the prior described Prospect Place in Dresden OH), and Marysville attesting to the citizens' enthusiastic commitment to their secular freedom, and pointing to their determination to keep the law in the hands of the people. As for me, having grown up in Southern Germany, I was used to seeing

86

churches dominating the towns' centers, indicating a reverence to the almighty God and His Law. This comparison might not be so far fetched: some Ohio County Courthouses are crowned with a figure representing the goddess of justice (reminiscent of the influence Roman law and religious culture had on the culture of the 19th century).

From Marietta we hurried back to our campsite at the Ohio River to claim a tent place. When we arrived there, the repairs on the main were completed, and we were allowed to pick a nice tenting site. The ground was dry, flat, shady, and covered with a well-groomed lawn, promising a good night's sleep. There was a friendly, middle-aged couple assigned to the campground as hosts. For its volunteer work, the National Forest Service allowed it to camp on the grounds throughout the season for free. The women did the cleaning of the facilities and cut the lawns, whereas the man kept the facilities in good repair. Both spent some time in front of our tent to chat with us.

"I have seen you guys before," the man claimed. "I saw your motorcycles last year in Newport, and then again yesterday on SR 26." What an amazing memory and how true it was. We did drive through Newport and visited the campground in October last year but believed then that there was nobody there to see us. We also drove on SR 26 yesterday in our search for a campsite. However, there must be thousands of motorcycles touring through the area each year. Perhaps we were the only ones with a green sidecar.

Tired from all the driving, tent setting, cooking, and talking, I laid down on the well groomed grass next to the tent and slept for an hour or two while Jonathan, who had actually done all the tent building and cooking, explored the foot trails around the camp area. Later in the evening, we watched coal-carrying barges on the river floating by or camp sight. Four to six of them were always tied closely together and pushed down the Ohio River by an amazingly quiet, Diesel-powered tugboat. Then we thought it might be nice to explore the opposite, West Virginia side of the river. Therefore, we drove north along the Ohio bank of the river for some 20 miles but there was no bridge crossing the river. Driving back through the little town of New Matamoras, we thought it would be good to celebrate with some beer before we go to sleep, but there was none sold in the little general store at the roadside. So, we returned to the campground and called it a sober night as the public campsite requires.

The next morning, a deep humming woke me from a wonderfully relaxing night's sleep. From the cowboy films of my youth, I remembered that Indian guides could feel or hear with their ears to the ground the approach of the enemy, or a train, or a buffalo herd long before they arrived. The vibration in the ground this morning came from approaching river barges that passed our campground. In spite of their enormous load of many hundred tons of coal, they traveled hushed, as if not to annoy the people along the riverbanks. The tugboats' diesel engines sounded off this deep-tone humming. I felt it on our tent floor more than I heard it just like those Indians did then. The sight and sound of the riverboats are reminders of a time that brought much wealth to those Ohioans who had settled along the waterways.

During a short breakfast, we ate Elsa's homemade granola bars and planned a route for our return to home. Jonathan suggested that we leave Marietta via SR 550 and follow it westward until Bartlett where we would meet SR 555 which leads northwest toward a tiny little settlement, called Portersville. There, he suggested, we turn onto SR 37, which would guide us further northwest into Westerville and home.

SR 555 turned out to be the most awesome road I had ever traveled by motorcycle. Leading along top ridges of the Appalachians, it climbed up and down numerous hills in seemingly endless curves winding around woods, pastures, and few farmhouses. Scenic foot trails crossed our road every now and then.

We were alone on that road at that time of the week and day. There was no Saturday morning traffic. There was no crop farming left or right and we saw no farming equipment on the road or in the fields. Wooded and grassy knolls characterized the constantly changing scenery. A few cattle grazed the pastures here and there. Few, single standing farm houses were spread over the 30-mile stretch between Bartlett and Portersville. It took two hours of high intensity driving and gazing into the beauty of this Ohio landscape. So many sites would have pleased me to live there the rest of my life, but where would I shop groceries, or fill my gasoline tank, get my cars serviced, or receive emergency medical care? I may have become too much accustomed to and even dependent on the convenience of living in town.

In Portersville, a village not much more than a junction of two county roads, we took a rest at the only gas station and eatery, and ordered a quick lunch. While we were sitting there, two or three large packs of Harley Davidson motorcyclists passed by, refueled, and left in the direction from where we had come. Were they not good evidence, that our road discovery also met their biking taste? One team of three middle-aged riders on three different brands of large sporty motorcycles, came back, entered the restaurant, sat next to us, ordered their lunch, and invited some conversation. They said they were from York, and that they were out for a Saturday pleasure trip. After a short loop on SR 555 they said, they had decided that it was too hilly for them. I had an urge to ask where York was but I did not want to expose my ignorance or hurt their feelings. I only knew of the stately town of York in England with its rich history, but I was sure that they were not from England since they spoke with the local, southern Ohio accent. Later at home, I Goggled for York in Ohio and found one. Located in Tuscarawas County near the New Philadelphia-Dover metro area it indicated a population of 1,292 and was about 100 miles straight north from where we ate with them in Portersville's gasoline station. They must have traveled for at least 100 miles already and may have been too tired to tackle another exhausting stretch of rollercoaster but gorgeous riding.

The remaining trip home on SR 37 was less exciting but helped me wind down, to think of getting home safely, and to listen to the performance of my motorcycle. A heavy wind had started to blow from southwest into our sides and it made my driving a little more challenging. I needed to steer strongly to the left to maintain a forward direction. Later, when I discussed this with Jonathan he said that he only needed to lean against the force of the wind – another difference between solo motorcycle riding and rig driving.

During our three-day trip, we had traveled about 350 miles on state and county roads with great pleasure and without harm to us or to our motorcycles. We had learned more about beautiful landscapes in Ohio and should look forward to more sightseeing and camping trips in the future. We arrived home at 4 PM, just in time to change dress and meet with our Columbus children for a joint Saturday evening dinner.

Serpent Mound In Adams County, Southern Ohio

Serpent Mound spreads over the top of a crater plateau, overlooking the Brush Creek Valley of Ohio's Adams County and SR 73 passes by it, south of Hillsboro. It is an astounding reminder of America's prehistoric Indians. Serpent Mound is a dirt mound piled up three feet high above the terrain, thirty feet wide, and 1,348 feet long. According to the guesses of experts, it depicts an uncoiling serpent wiggling northward, with its mouth wide open, trying to swallow a massive egg. The head of the serpent is aligned with the summer solstice sunset and the coils point to the winter solstice sunrise and the equinox sunrise. Of course, the exact meaning or purpose of the figure is not known and many interpretations have been suggested. However, everything points to a religious effigy, rather then to burial places.

Excavations at Serpent Mound in 1996 revealed no burials but wood charcoal was found. Unfortunately, cultural artifacts have not been found within the Serpent Mound. The contours of the mound can bee seen on this website photo, as well as walking paths that lead the tourists around the mound without getting their feet wet.

The Serpent Mound (Pollinator at en.wikipedia).

Indian culture and history has always interested me and in previous years, Gudrun and I had visited other mounds near Newark, Chillicothe, and Dayton. Therefore, when Jonathan suggested a motorcycle trip to Serpent Mound I was excited. Again, we used one of Jonathan's free Fridays to plan a day's visit to Serpent Mound.

90

At the beginning of our trip we took SR 62, which covered the flatland between Columbus, Washington Courthouse, and Hillsboro, and it took little more than an hour. From Hillsboro we took SR 73 further south and the landscape became increasingly more hilly and exciting to see. After Loudon, good signage at the roadside pointed to the state Memorial Serpent Mound. A steep driveway, off SR 73 and to the left wound around a conical hill and entered into the park. We arrived there at about 11 AM and the sun had just started to warm up the terrain. The park was beautifully laid out and well manicured (see on the picture of the mount). At first, we were all alone and spent one hour walking around the serpent. We climbed up a watchtower, took photographs (see above), read every sign there was about the mound, visited a little museum in a typical, picturesque stone house of the state park style (called *"parkeresque"* by the ranger there), and learned a few more historical cues on the life of the Adena Indians and the Fort Ancient culture.

What excited me most in our postmodern time was the fact, that these two Indian cultures, considered to be involved in the evolution of this site, left nothing behind about them selves, except their apparent reverence for their gods. It seems that their snake effigy had religious meaning just as the passes of the sun and the moon may have had to them. They left nothing more to us.

Almost 4000 years later, we marvel about these extensive earth works, which the Indians must have created with their bare hands and Stone Age tools, without the help of wheels or beasts of burden, and they may have piled up dirt for many years, without expecting economical benefits. What other power could have convinced those people to labor so hard for no personal gain? Was it their respect or their fear of their gods? For us now, their earthworks characterize their culture, just as their poetry, art, dance, and music would have done if any such information had been found for us to study.

The Fort Ancient culture disappeared by 1550 AD, at a time when religious strife raged in Europe, when North America was conquered by European immigrants, who escaped the religious intolerance of their home countries, but then they squeezed the American Indians gradually out of their land and casually destroyed their culture by their religious, racial, and cultural intolerance.

Adams County has many cultural memorials just like the Serpent Mound. For that reason only, and also considering the scenic routes of SR 73 and 41, we should plan to visit that county again.

The End of The Rig

For three years now the rig had been under my care. The many worries about its mechanical integrity, the books and websites I consulted, the repairs I pursued, the many trips I took, and, last but not least, the special fellowship it fostered between me and my third son-in-law, Jonathan, all were well worth this investment.

Jonathan determines the next part of a trip, 2008.

Jonathan had joined my family in 2006 when he married my youngest daughter Elsa. Besides a wonderful husband to Elsa, he became an enjoyable companion and friend to me. A mechanical engineer and BMW fan, he was a respectful and interested listener who gladly contributed to our joint hobby of motorcycles. He had a dry, language related humor and often knowledgeable and constructive opinions on alternative solutions. He was willing to lead a project or a trip whenever he saw a need. He traveled with me on many short and some long distance trips, and we both enjoyed them for the mere sake of riding powerful, comfortable, reliable, well designed, and age- tested motorcycles.

With time, however, I developed a preoccupation with everything related to the rig. I engaged in that hobby just as I had done with my academic career: full power and full time. Daily, I scanned the web for BMW related, technical information. I read books on the principles of Otto engines and on the specifics of boxer engines. I collected information on how to diagnose troubles, and how to prevent them. I compared motorcycle models and assessed their technical advantages and disadvantages. In short, I spent many hours every day on the computer just as I had done the previous 35 years while working for my former passion, the field of biomaterials. Day and night, I pondered about the next action to be taken. When would an oil change be due and what other proactive care should be done at the same time? Do I have the tools to remove and replace the oil filter? What are the symptoms of a loose front end and would there be special tools and parts available for my custom front fork? Should I have my own trailer that can transport the entire rig in case it breaks down somewhere on the road? Is the engine noise indicative of worn bearings? Where could I travel to next?

I had taken many motorcycle on tours around town and increasingly further through the country for half days, full days, and even two or three days. Beyond issues related to the motorcycle, I learned how Ohio's history repeatedly molded its economy; I marbled about the coming and going of societal wealth and its effect on the urban and rural landscape. It was a pleasure to travel on today's remarkably well-maintained national, state, and county roads in Ohio and I concluded that this state had invested wisely in its road network and thus in its economical future.

Gudrun and Elsa' often questioned me: "What is so enjoyable about a motorcycle?" The first answer in my mind was always that I just liked motorcycles. However, what was it specifically that I liked? Are motorcycles and especially rigs not an anachronism among modern means of transportation? Today's alternatives bring us from one place to another with greater comfort, safer, dryer, warmer, quieter, and, in general, better isolated from the side effects of the engine, the road, and the weather. In light of all of these indisputable facts, my main reason could not be merely the quality of transportation or less costly transportation, even though I often used those arguments as my chief defense. On purpose, I drove the rig to work, went shopping, and met all my appointments throughout the year, provided, that the motorcycle was in driving condition and the road free of snow and ice. What then were my reasons for owning a motorcycle?

When I saw my three-year-old grandson Evan riding on our little tricycle (see Figure 1) around a flowerbed in our backyard patio again and again, I wondered, what it was that made him do this? One day I saw another grandson, less than three years old, lying on his belly and pushing little matchbox cars around the carpet while mimicking engine noises with his voice, different noises for different model cars. What was his motives? Although I cannot give answers for those boys, I believe for myself, however, that it is the thrill of being in control, to build and operate engines, to drive them safely or competitively, perhaps sub-conscientiously, to master their power and inherent dangers. There are even sensual stimuli to the motorcyclist that trigger pleasurable emotions. I can think of the humming noise of the running engine, the sweet smell of engine oil, the head wind blowing into my face, the passing of other vehicles, the hands-on tuning and repair activities around a sophisticate engine, and the uplifting feeling when eventually the engine is running well. It could also be answering of admirers' questions. Can that be it? For a boy, all these feelings can lead to wholesome activities and preparations toward their career, in my case surgery and biomedical engineering. However, what does it do to a retired man? I do remember that the rig was actually planned as a retirement occupation, and that it was to be a fulfilling hobby.

Eventually, however, my rig became a demon to me and it competed with my love for Christ and His church, for my wife and our life together, and for my children and their relationship with me? How could I have gotten so enthralled with it in this stage of life?

One night then, I decided to give up this idol. I sold the rig while it was still in good driving condition. In order to get back what I had invested, I had set the asking price at $8,000 and advertised the rig in various media. There was The Internet BMW Riders with its excellent, nationwide advertising. There was the sidecar community with its specialized advertising of rigs, and then there was the local Craig's list.

The first round of adds in early March had brought no responses. Perhaps it was too early in the season. A second ad in late March brought three or four responses, apparently from BMW fans, since they seemed mostly interested in pictures and how my BMW motorcycle and sidecar were fitted together. Craig's list readers only wanted to know what my final price would be without asking for any technical details. Of course, there were a good number of Internet schemes, offering to pay for the motorcycle and the shipping before serious questions were asked, or the rig inspected. For a third round of adds in late May, I reduced the asking price to $7,000. The biking season was in full swing and I received four serious responses.

The first of those callers was so excited on the phone that he did not even want to know details of the rig. He said he was familiar with the K100 and had restored a number of BMW motorcycles before. He immediately sent a down payment and came as he had promised two weeks later from Wisconsin with a brand-new, closed cabin trailer. He paid in cash, loaded up the rig and left, all within an hour. To the other three interested persons I sent an e-mail of regret, for which they actually thanked me in return e-mails. After almost a year of agonizing whether I was making the right decision, now I was actually glad that it sold. The final selling price seemed appropriate for what I had spent for its purchase ($6,000) and repairs ($3,000). I calculated that in three years I lost $2,000 as depreciation. It also felt good that the motorcycle was in good mechanical condition and that I did not need to praise the motorcycle beyond its worth. Above all, however, I thanked God for his protection throughout these past three years. Thanks to him, there were no accidents or injuries to either Jonathan or me. Physically unharmed, we returned to our loving wives.

But then, Gudrun and Elsa felt that the best for me would be to buy another motorcycle now, perhaps smaller, or a trike so I could not tip over when stopping at traffic lights. Thinking about their suggestion, As a veterinarian, I had used this very same psychology often for mourning clients who had lost their beloved pet. A new puppy, I always thought, would help heal the pain of their loss. Yet, in this case, I was sure, that the rig phase of my life had been completed.

What was left to do was to record my memories so I would have something to talk about to my grandsons Evan, Hendrik, Alexander, Titus, or Konrad when they come and visit their grandfather who used to ride a motorcycle. Perhaps they will someday dream of owning a motorcycle themselves. Or they will just brag to their friends how their old grandfather used to operate a motorcycle with a sidecar, at a time when cars were controlled by computer chips, to park neatly next to the sidewalk, to start the windshield wipers on their own when the first raindrops fall onto the windshield, to open or close the car top automatically while driving, or prevent the car from tipping over in sharp bends. Perhaps they will mention the extra gas tank attached to the rear end of the motorcycle for safety on long trips.

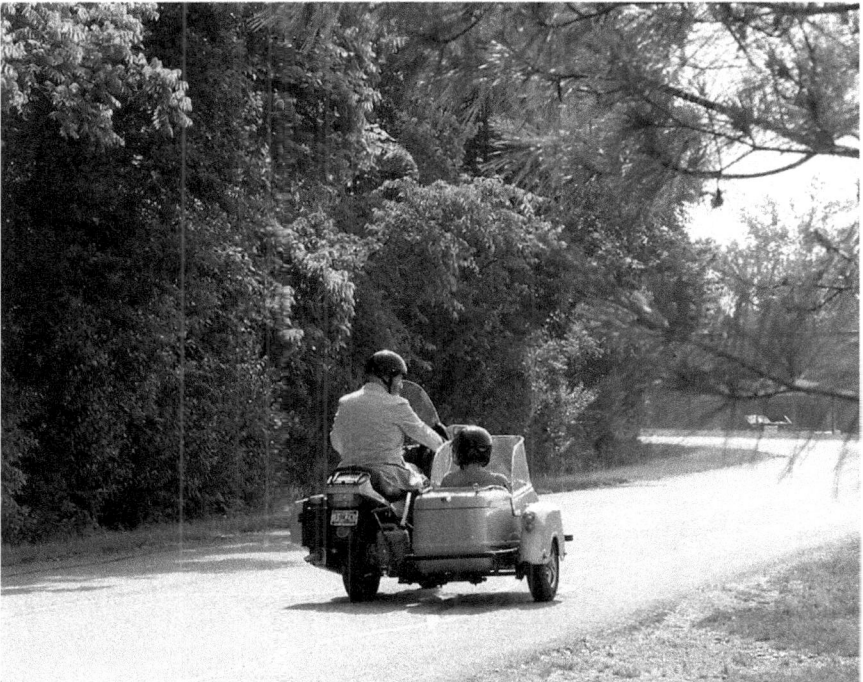

My Beautiful Past-time Occupation, 2007.

The Honda PC 800 Motorcycle

It was September 9, 2009 when the green BMW rig sold. I had grown fond of it. It was powerful and sturdy. Its bulky sidecar was handy to hold the motorcycle upright, and to store clothing, tools, shopping, and camping stuff in it. Yet, perhaps because of the progressing age of the motorcycle I had spent too much time and emotions solving small and big problems that arose all the time. The motorcycle needed many replacement procedures and many sidecar alignments. There was specifically one major repair that still needed to be done: Although the transmission and final drive were replaced, an overhaul of the engine or its replacement was the next big and necessary task to be undertaken.

With the motorcycle I myself was aging as well. Increasing weakness of my legs made it more strenuous to push the rig backward out of the shed and turn it around on the gravel driveway before I could ride it. Another final reason to sell the rig was the fact that my wife Gudrun did not ever enjoy coming along in the sidecar and there was therefore no good justification for having the sidecar which only increased gasoline consumption from a projected solo-motorcycle use of 45 mpg to a many times tested 27 mpg. Luckily, the rig found its new owner. I phoned him six months later and he sent me a nice photo riding the rig and his teenage daughter sitting in the sidecar. It makes me happy that the rig found a new enthusiastic owner.

All throughout the subsequent fall and winter I looked for an alternative hobby. Because of my weak legs, I would not have wanted another heavy motorcycle and all BMW road motorcycles weigh 450 lbs. and more, with high seats that made it enormously difficult for me to swing my right leg over the seat. A trike would have been a nice alternative. There were kits that one could buy to attach a set of two wheals to the rear of any big motorcycle. This kit would make the motorcycle free standing and would allow easier mounting, but the costs of such a rigged motorcycle in those days would have been in the lower twenties. Another alternative would have been a trike from can-am called Spyder. It looks like a cross of a car (with two permanently installed front wheels) and a snowmobile. It also reminded me of the Messerschmitt vehicle that I experienced in my teenage years. The Spyder even has a reverse gear so I would not have to push it out of the shed or the parking space. I eventually discarded that idea because the Spyder was an all-new product and its price of $19-25 K was outside of my retirement budget. I looked at smaller BMW motorcycles of the past, such as the R60 or R50/5 like the one I used to own in the seventies and eighties. Our local BMW parts dealer Re-Psycle in Lithopolis had plenty of used motorcycles in that class prized at around $5,000. But I was hesitant to buy another motorcycle that would need constant adjustments or even mayor repairs sooner than later while I myself was aging fast. All these considerations toned down my desire, to own another motorcycle.

But then, a neighbor in our street had a Honda Pacific Coast 800, which she did not drive. It had only been ridden 12,00 miles by a previous owner, a man of my age. After a pleasant test drive I bought it for $2,000. Now, it was even heavier than the BMW motorcycles. It weighed 650 lbs. and it was challenging to push it out of my shed. But it had a significantly lower seat and was easy for me to mount. Its beauty was its riding comfort, perhaps due to its low point of gravity.

It had all the power I would have wanted — perhaps even more. It gave a soft and comfortable ride with almost no engine or exhaust noise, and it was completely enclosed in soft shell Tupperware-like plastic fairing, which helped to maintain a neat and clean appearance. Most of all, the price for this well maintained and little used motorcycle was so low that I felt comfortable to buy it, drive it for another year or two, and then, when appropriate, sell it again without great loss. It was March 2009 when I bought it and by then at least in my mind the motorcycle season had begun. To myself I promised that this would only be an ordinary motorcycle and not a dream.

Through many, many little trips within and around Columbus's metropolitan area I learned to handle this big motorcycle such as lifting it onto its center stand, driving narrow circles and turns, planting both my feet down onto the road surface when stopping at traffic lights, raising my feet up high to the footrests quickly when starting to drive, revving the engine when downshifting gears, or pushing the heavy motorcycle backward out of parking or the shed without dropping it. Then I dared bigger tours, some of them with, and many others without the company of Jonathan my son-in-law.

Plott Days In Holmes County, East Central Ohio

Two or three years earlier, I had met Jackie Carpenter at a dog show at the fairgrounds in Columbus, OH. She showed Plott hounds. She said she breeds Beagles and Plott hounds and she also judges hounds. She lived near Gambier, Ohio, about 50 miles north of Columbus and 5 miles east of Mt. Vernon. I asked whether I could come and visit her kennel some day. She hesitated a little before she agreed. She was worried, she said, since there was nothing exciting to be seen at her place.

In the early spring of 2010 I phoned Jackie Carpenter and she agreed that my wife Gudrun and I could come that very day, and so we went there by car. It was a cold day and a little wet snow was on the ground. Her place was on a side branch off the county road. The tiny house was only a few feet off the road and a semi truck was parked next to it. In front of the house's entry door was a beautiful, one, or two-year old Plott female, chained to a peg in the ground. She was a very elegant Plott type, slender, high off the ground and with a dark and shiny mahogany color with dark brindle on it. I fell in love with that dog right away. Mrs. Carpenter had awaited us and came out of the house immediately. But because wet snow was falling, Gudrun stayed in the car. Mrs Carpenter explained that the female, temporarily chained in front of the house, was normally kept inside and was her show dog; the other hounds would be in her backyard and they were hunters.

We walked a few yards behind her house, down a few yards on a graveled path and there were seven hounds. Three Plott hounds were chained to their peg in the ground with a swivel joint. Three Beagles were accommodated in little kennels, and than there was a female Bluetick Coonhound of the smaller type in her own small kennel. She sat on her doghouse and barked the entire time we were there. All the hounds were of the hunting type, smaller than show dogs, and lean from being regularly hunted. Mrs. Carpenter said that it was mostly her husband Jim who hunted them whenever he was home. I asked her if she could alert me by e-mail when there was a hound show in the vicinity and she said she would. Then Gudrun and I left for Mt. Vernon, a nice little town.

Almost 9 month later, Mrs. Carpenter sent a message, saying that there would be the National Plott Hound Association's Plott Days near Holmesville, not far from her home. She sent me the advertising of the association, and weeks later the description of how to get there. I marked my calendar for August 5-7 and planned to attend. For August 5th excellent weather was forecasted and I saw this as a rare opportunity to combine my hunting, hounds, and motorcycle hobbies to visit the Plott Days. If I had not removed the radio from my motorcycle, I even could have added my love for music and listen to classical music during that 2 hours trip.

The Plott Days are a gathering of like-minded people who breed, hunt, and show Plott Hounds. During those days they gather on a camp ground, socialize with each other and their hounds, tell stories of "the best hound they ever had", show them in a little bench show gathering, have raccoon hunting trials at night, and sometimes even bear hunting trials. I had attended such a day many years ago. My youngest son Thomas was 5 years old at that time and accompanied me to that gathering. We had taken three of our own Plotts with us and we all had great fun there, especially with the tame bear that someone had brought for the trials.

This year's meeting was on the grounds of a local hunting club, which fitted the needs of the Plott Days well. In the middle of a perhaps one acre large clearing there was an open shed, which provided shade to tables and benches, ideal for a small scale bench showing. There was also a hut for the business affairs of the meeting, and there were a few dealers who offered hunting dog paraphernalia out of their trailers.

The site was about 80 miles from Columbus OH, a good 2 hours motorcycle riding. I arrived at about 11 AM and people were still setting up their camps. The site was west of State Rout 83, and further west of a railway line (parallel and left to Hwy 83), and then off Township Rout 559 to the north. The woods around it, tugged away from mayor road traffic, seemed an ideal place for raccoon hunting.

There were about thirty pickup trucks parked at that time of the day and most were lined up along the edges of the clearing.

102

Some people had set up their trailers, others erected tents, and a few had signed into local motels and stayed only during daytime. May be about 100 Plott hounds and a few coonhounds of other breeds were chained to pegs in the ground lined up along the edge of the woods, most of them behind the pickup trucks in the deep shade of the trees and the cars.

I parked my motorcycle on a little, graveled spot close to the center of the activities, walked around between the campers, and looked at all the hounds. I also talked with some of the people about the physical appearance of the Plotts of today as compared to the time of my involvement 25 years ago. Although today's Plott hounds were as elegant and beautiful as I fondly remember them, I now observed that the majority of Plotts were standing higher on their legs and were built more slender than they used to be. Also, their fur color had darkened and many of the hounds appeared to be almost black. Only when the son light shone on them one could see the brindle striping especially along the inside of their legs. Another observation was, that very many of the younger hounds were extremely shy and timid. Now, it might be that they were raised in the backyard for hunting purposes and had not yet been exposed to many people. But I do not remember such shyness from Plott hounds of my earlier years of involvement in South Carolina[7]. One of the directors, I believe his name was Johnny Gibson from Alabama, kindly introduced himself and stood with me for a while. So, we talked a little about the changes in the breed that I observed. Although he agreed to the physical changes, he felt that they would not matter much to the Plott hound people since their hounds are bred for hunting ability and not so much for appearance. Although his statement may be a true reflection of many of the Plott hound hunters, there are the conformation shows going on even at that meeting, and the Plott hound breed had just been accepted by the AKC for its shows.

---

[7] Andreas F. von Recum, *Hunting with Hounds in North America*, Pelican Publ., 2002).

A typical brindle Plott Coonhound, 2010.

Also, the peculiar dark brindle color is one of the striking differences to other Coonhound breeds. In fact, the Plott Hound breeding associations do not register any other colors but brindle, which sounds to me that color is considered a critical characteristic of this hound breed, whether it is germane to the hunting quality or not. In fact, when there are buckskin (yellow) puppies born within a purebred brindle litter, those puppies are not acceptable for registration, or showing. I doubt that their color expresses a differrent hunting ability.

When I had seen all dogs, talked with a few owners, and watched some last minute training for showing, it was time for me to head back home. While I tried to mount my motorcycle, it slipped away from under me on the gravel and then fell on me, burying my left leg under it. Immediately two or three men were there and lifted my motorcycle and me up again. Full of concern, they investigated us both for visible damage. Since there was none, they helped me back into the saddle and bid me fare well. They may have wondered whether I was still fit for motorcycle riding, and what had brought me to their Plott hound meet? I however left with a revival of my love for Plott hounds and what beautiful hunting hounds they really were.

104

Along the Ohio River

Jonathan and I took a long-planned trip to Ohio's East side again. This time, we planned to stay on the road for three days and pitch or tent the first night at Harrison State Park, north of the village of Cadiz.

Cadiz in Harrison County, East Central Ohio

While preparing for this trip, I could find very little historical information about Cadiz and some of what I know now, I learned from the owner or manager of an eatery on Court Street in Cadiz, a few minutes walking distance from the village center and County Court House.

Cadiz is located about 25 miles west of Steubenville Ohio. A rural center and at the same time, the administrative seat of Harrison County, Cadiz sits where highways 250, 9, and 22 intersect with each other. It was established in 1803, at the same time when many other Ohio settlements were also started such as Worthington, my hometown. Its residents named the village after the Spanish city of Cadiz. According to Wikipedia, its residents manufactured goods and processed the crops of farmers from the surrounding countryside. In 2000, Cadiz had a population 3,308 people.

Some famous men originated in Cadiz: There was the well-known movie actor Clark Gable. Then, there was the Methodist Bishop Matthew Simpson. He was not only an influential clergyman and church leader, but also a professor and president of a university and later a seminary. He was a close, personal, and trusted friend of President Abraham Lincoln, who considered his advice of great value. That is why Bishop Simpson attended the family at Lincoln's death and gave the sermon at his funeral in Springfield. There was also the republican Congress Man John Bingham who served as judge advocate in the trial of the Lincoln assassination. He was prosecutor in the impeachment trials of Andrew Johnson, and was also principal framer of the Fourteenth Amendment to the United States Constitution. It is amazing to me how citizens of this little village connected so intimately to the central history of this nation.

From an architectural point of view I found a few pearls. Like so many other courthouses in Ohio, the Harrison County Court House was built 1895 during the period of Eclecticism a time of many stylistic revivals, when especially courthouses were built in the Graeco-Roman Classical style. I saw the pride of the people in their legal system symbolized in the broad front staircase leading to their judiciary. As one can notice, however, the prominent, stately front stairway was no longer in use, perhaps because the stairs were decaying and unsafe to use, or because there is little influence left to this remote county seat.

Harrison County Court House, 2010.

There may be an elevator accessible through one of the side doors, so that the court employees and court customers are not always covered in sweat when arriving for their court business.

We had parked our motorcycles in front of the county's political party offices across the street from the courthouse. The republican office was on the right, and the democratic next to it one on the left.

Our motorcycles parked next to political party offices, 2010.

Most of the buildings along Court Street were of the same revival period. Next to the party offices was another Graeco-Roman Classical house with some renaissance influence, which may have been a bank building at an earlier time. Classical-style ornaments were incorporated into the red brick façade.

The fronts of all the houses on that street were well cared for but the best maintained building façade belonged to a corner building. It was erected in Colonial Revival or a mixed revival style; peculiar were the white horn-shaped upper corners of the windows. And inscription in gilded letters on a black band above the door read: Rosebud Mining Company. It may be one of the last signs of a once productive coalmining county.

While we were eating lunch downtown, we asked our waitress for driving directions to the campground in the Harrison State Park. Very friendly, she gave us detailed and easy to understand directions and wished us well on our vacation tour. Unfortunately, when we followed her advise we detected that there was a bridge construction on State Rout 9 that would lead to the State Park, and we were directed onto some bypasses. We ended up on gravel roads crisscrossing the top of the hills of the State Park.

107

Loose gravel on the road forced us to ride extremely slowly and cautiously.

Interestingly, a young man with whom we had a short talk on this gravel road, gave us further directions and then he warned us that he had totaled his motorcycle on that very road and that we should be riding carefully. Minutes later, and in spite of his warnings and our cautiousness both our bikes slid at a steep decline of the road, where the gravel was lying especially deep. Both our motorcycles fell over simultaneously and next to each other. Luckily, nothing bad happened to our bodies. My Honda however, received some damage to the left side of its fairing, and to the left rear mirror which had broken off. Less than one minute later, another young man who came up the hill stopped his pickup truck in front of us, helped us to get back onto our feet, and to lift up our motorcycles. Jonathan then walked my motorcycle down the steep slope for about 30 yards and set it up on its side stand there. Then he walked back up the hill, and guided his own motorcycle down as well. After a short inspection of our motor-cycles, and when my legs had stopped shaking, we dared to ride on, but the damage on my Honda dampened my enthusiasm for quite a while.

Eventually, we arrived at our destination, a tiny little, *primitive campground*. Nobody was camping there, or came to charge us for camping. A huge, old-fashioned, hand operated pump delivered plenty of water that was, however declared unsui-table for drinking. There was also a toilet, but no hand washbasins. Still we enjoyed the remoteness and quietness of the location and stayed there for the night. Throughout the night I had hoped for the sounds of coonhounds hunting in the woods, but only a few, far away house dogs barked themselves into their sleep. Perhaps there was no hunting season yet, or no coons to run.

Next morning we packed up and left for church service in Steubenville, 25 miles to the east from our campsite. Since it took us longer than expected to get down to State Rt. 22 we reached the Steubenville Church unfortunately in time to hear the concluding prayer.

The most memorable impression of Steubenville was its ubiquitous smell of bituminous coal, just as I remembered how the entire East Germany had smelled before its political collapse in 1989. The heydays of Steubenville, according to its website, were

108

in the 1940 ties – 60 ties when coal mining and the steel and manufacturing industry were booming. Its strategic location at the waterways of the Ohio River and the railways connecting Pittsburg with Cincinnati, St. Louis, and Chicago were important economical assets for this river town. Steubenville's population, once 20,000 residents, is now the fastest declining population of any urban area in the US because of the rapid disappearance of job opportunities. Later I read in the newspaper, that the town had given up planning for growth in order to stop the bleeding. When we were there on Sunday Morning, the early sun favored the west sides of the streets and created stark contrasts to the shady east side of buildings. The town looked eerily empty but we still enjoyed unhindered gliding in the morning light through the business area that appeared deserted from modern economy. There were empty factory plants left and right along the river which stemmed from the industrial boom of the late 19th and early 20th century. Their dark brown-red brick walls were weathered from the many years of coal fire smog. Many of their windows were smashed, and trash filled their yards.

We were not really looking out for architectural pearls, but then, while riding on SR 7 along the relicts of former industriousness, in the middle of town, we passed an interesting building complex which dominated the junction of Dean Martin Boulevard and Logan Street. Its gently curving walls toward SR 7 were reminiscent of the American Deco, a building style of the late 1930 ties. Light ochre, glazed, clean tiles on the east walls shone up brightly in the morning sun.

By the way, the name Steubenville had a good ring in my German ears and I had been looking forward to seeing this town. The name reminded me of the Steuben Society of America, which was founded in New York in 1919 to foster cultural friendships between the people of post-WWI Germany and the USA. After WWII this society became even more instrumental in maintaining camaraderie between both Nations and their governments. Did that society relate to the German-American General Friedrich Wilhelm von Steuben who fought on General Washington's side, or did it relate to the town and people of Steubenville (which, by the way, was named in honor of said general)? I found it especially sad to see the economic decline of this city, while Germany's economy, in general, has been doing so well for many decades.

Not far from downtown we turned right, off SR 7 and onto SR 22. We left Steubenville and the State of Ohio, by crossing over the river to the east, and entered West Virginia. On that side of the river we turned right again and followed State Rt. 2 southward along the riverbank for the next 100 miles.

The Ohio River between West Virginia and Ohio

On our trip southward along the Ohio River, we had sunshine all the way. We passed through little towns and industrial plants that spread out next to and along the riverbanks where they must have been benefitting from the closeness of the shipping route on land and on the water. We passed by a number of active power plants where large white smoke columns rose straight up into the blue sky and could be seen many miles ahead.

On the west side across the river, the Ohio side, we saw mostly vegetation-covered banks hiding settlements and industrial sites behind that green curtain. Empty barges bundled in sixes or even nines traveled down the river, and coal filled barges were shoved up the river but much slower because of their load and opposing current. All this scenery was bathed in bright sunshine. Few, white clouds chased along the light blue sky. The temperature was perfect for motorcycle riding ranging between 68 and 78 °F. There was almost no road traffic to divert our attention from the scenery. We could not have picked a better day for this sight-seeing tour along the impressive Ohio River, the main transporttation artery of Ohio's early settlers.

At a Mexican style fastfood place still on the West Virginia side of the river we stopped for lunch. While we ate a Hamburger with a Mexican name we changed our trip plans and aimed at the Leigh Run State Campground on the Ohio side for our next night's accommodation. That campground was 25 miles north of Marietta, directly on State Rt. 7. Twice before, we had been there and liked its ambiance. At this time of the year, the only customers on the campground were senior citicens traveling in RVs who enjoyed the serenity of the river and the amenities of electricity and piped water. Some of these people had grandchildren who played ball on the well groomed grounds. But there were also "primitive" sites for tent campers and they were most afordable for our needs. After

110

we had set up our tent we decided to pay another visit to the beautiful little town of Marietta which we had already seen twice before.

Marietta in Washington County, Southeast Ohio

The main street architectural mixture of styles which I saw in Marietta's downtown fascinated me, just like I had observed it in so many other Ohio towns that I had visited before.

Main street in Marietta, Ohio, 2010.

The house on the very right of our photo, almost opposite of the courthouse (not seen here), shows features of classical revival, but as one can see, the other houses to the left, although they all may have been built within the same dozen of years, their façades represented very different and simpler revival styles. The immediate neighboring house showed Ibero-Islamic reminiscent tile decorations above the top windows. The immediate next house in bright white reminded me of Italianate, Romantic houses as I

111

had seen them first in Ripley in southern Ohio at the northern banks of the Ohio River. Next to them are three houses with a Victorian-Queen Ann appearance, and at the end of the street was a church being of the Gothic Revival style. It imitated the original Gothic churches to such a degree that even the tower was uncompleted, just as all originally gothic towers of the 13th century had remained unfinished because the peoples' worldview had changed into the very different Renaissance. I learned later, that all these styles used here in the 19th century are merely treatments of the exterior for their esthetic – good appearance but are not accompanied by differing internal construction principles or techniques.

It was a hot Sunday afternoon and only few tourists — like we — strolled along the downtown streets. By 5:30 PM we rode back to the campground, built a fire, cooked a meal, and turned into our tent to escape the mosquitoes eagerly searching for tourists' blood.

Our return trip home was uneventful. Altogether we had driven 500 miles through Ohio's most beautiful but poorest regions, the weather was kind to us during those three days and the Lord protected us from all harm.

Main Street Architecture

During my many sightseeing trips I grew fond of the downtown or "Main Street", appearance of the many towns I passed through. So I started to plan trips just to visit and photograph downtowns. Delaware, a neighboring town some 10 miles north of Worthington is one good example. I have driven there many times because it has the pleasant appearance of a county seat and university town.

Downtown Delaware, 2011.

Delaware impressed me with its well-maintained center, especially when I saw it again and again! Only the traffic lights and the imposing, oversized optometrist's store sign detracted me from this picture of Delaware's better past. Again, I was fascinated and at the same time puzzled by the many different façades of the commercial-residential houses even though most of them were built within the same few decades of the 19th century. They document a time when store facades spoke of individual investment in the beauty of the community's downtown. But what were the reasons for this variety of architectural styles? First, I tried to

113

find a book, which would help me identify the architectural styles. The one that helped me best was: *"A Field Guide to American Houses"*[8]. My son–in-law John kindly gave it to me for Christmas 2010 and I read up on Ohio's history to find explanations why Downtowns developed the way they did. Here is what I learned:

Although European immigrants during the 18th century traded with Native Americans in the Ohio territory, most did not actually settle down there until after the American Revolutionary War. When the Ohio territory was opened to settlement the initial immigrants were mostly farmers and so many rural towns developed early for their convenience. But then considerable immigration pressure evolved and within less than 40 years, by 1801 Ohio's population had reached 45,000. In 1803 Ohio became the 17th state of the Union.

The settlers were involved in farming, manufacturing, mining, and trading. To improve commerce, they supported the construction of the Ohio and Erie Canal. The resulting canals connected the river routes with the Great Lakes in the north and with the Mississippi Delta in the south. Through these routes great wealth was brought to settlements along the waterways and, as a result, towns evolved along them at that time. Farming products from the center and west of the state, but also iron ore and coal from the eastern counties near the Ohio River, as well as oil from the northeast supported fast trade expansions. The first Ohio town was Marietta, which was founded around 1788 at the confluence of the Muskingum with the Ohio River where it benefited greatly from river transports.

Then, triggered by the construction of the National Road (now I-40), which was completed in 1810, an ever-expanding road network spread over the state and soon improved long distance transportation of goods on land, and competed with the waterways. It connected Ohio to the east coast across the Appalachian Mountains. A new wave of settlements benefitted especially from this mode of transportation and the new wealth showed in the elaborate architecture of farm and town houses, and merchants houses downtown. Then, starting in 1836 the railways rapidly replaced the waterways as the dominant means of transportation.

---

[8] Virginia & Lee McAlester: A Field Guide to American Houses, Alfred A. Knopf, and New York, 2009.

New settlements shot up along the railroad tracks and larger cities evolved at railroad junctions. Large-scale industrial buildings appeared in the brick gothic style of those days.

Then, the trucking industry started in the mid 20th century, developed rapidly, and outperformed previous modes of transporttation because of its faster and more convenient goods delivery. As an unfortunate consequence or side effect settlements associated with the waterways and with the railroads lost their main source of income and faded away.

There were also waves of accumulation and decline of wealth following the mining of coal in the mid and southeast, manufacturing of steel in the Northeast, and mass production of field crops in the north and center of Ohio. All these changes have molded the local economy and with it the local culture, most visibly by its architecture. All of this happened within a short 230 years from about 1800 to 2009 when an USA- created financial crisis brought worldwide economy to the brink of collapse.

During the first 100 years of this short history of the State of Ohio's economy, Eclecticism was the prevailing architectural mood. The author of the book *Great Architecture of the World*, John Julius Norwich[9] said the following about Eclecticism: *"The 19th century was a time of enthusiastic and bewildering stylistic confusion" "leaving the battlefield strewn with architectural debris of every size, shape, color and style". "Styles were chosen not just for fashion but for their associative qualities: Roman for justice, Gothic for learning, Greek for government, Venetian for commerce, oriental for leisure, Hanseatic for housing. Every building told a story and pointed to a moral."*

Eclecticism dominated the building styles and appearance of 19th century American settlements. Newly rich Americans sought to emulate or even surpass the stature of the old rich Europeans. From their study of Europe and East Asia they turned with enthusiasm to the architecture of the Old World. Style elements from Greek, Roman, Near East and Far East, and English building periods were freely adapted to please the wealthy in Ohio –and probably elsewhere in the Americas. Here in downtown Delaware the Italianate style of Romantic houses seemed to prevail

---

[9] John Julius Norwich, Great Architecture of the World, Da Capo, London, 1975.

as judged by the hooded segmental arch details of the windows and the large eave brackets, which dominate the cornice line of Italianate houses.

Having grown up in Germany, I had learned there that architecture had set its markers of art onto specific historical time periods: Romanesque Medieval castles of the late first millennium AD, Gothic churches of the end of the 11th century, Renaissance buildings of the 13th to 16th century, or Baroque façades and churches in the 16th and 17th centuries, Classicism during the 18th and 19th century. In addition, each European nation and region had created its own modifications of these prevailing styles. The buildings became monuments for religion, economy, culture, and social conditions of the time in which the people lived then, the political struggles they experienced, and, of course, the wealth they invested in the arts.

With this, admittedly superficial and sketchy information on Ohio's historical, cultural, and economical background I now saw Main Streets in the light of the rise and decline of Ohio's past with all of its glory and pitfalls. During the late 19th and the beginning 20th century, Ohioans created world dominance in many industrial advances such as steel production, rubber manufacturing, car building, and chemical production. I am thinking of Ohio's industrial giants such as Rockefeller, Goodyear, Procter and Gamble, Edison, Sabin, and many others who revolutionized production and commercialization worldwide. Their wealth shows in the architecture of their days. Their private homes were often as magnificent, sometimes even bigger than residencies of European dukes. Their wealth was supportive or at least influential in the development of settlements with their often-lavish downtowns and magnificent public buildings such as the county courthouses. But a century later, unfortunately, some of that wealth had vanished and left many downtowns and their surrounding counties to decay. Poverty moved in and many downtowns and Main Streets fell unchecked into dormancy or even decay. The fate of Detroit and its relentless decay since the 1960 ties is a spooky topic in the news of 2013.

In my more recent sightseeing trips I focused my curiosity on Main Street commercial-residential buildings of the State of Ohio's first one hundred years, the 19th century. Surely, the downtown buildings of many of Ohio's towns speak of great wealth and

116

community pride of those days. Richard Longstreth in his book "The Buildings of Main Street"[10] called the downtown buildings of that time "two-part commercial block", and he said, "This type of building is the most common type of composition used for small and moderate-sized commercial buildings combined with residential uses throughout the country". A horizontal division into two zones characterizes it.

Two-Part Commercial Blocks in Delaware, 2011.

The lower zone is usually restricted to the ground floor and accommodates retail stores that offer products or services to the public. The upper zone, usually the floors above the ground floor were to facilitate offices, storage, or private residencies. This concept can be clearly seen in the three buildings shown here from Delaware. Nowadays, the upper floor windows are often blinded since nobody lives there anymore.

---

[10] The Preservation Press, Baltimore 1987.

Some of the storeowners show great pride in their building and its appearance. In one such building in Columbus beautifully arranged curtains show in the windows of the residential floor and perhaps there are people actually living on the upper floor.

In Europe the shop-house combination was the standard for Main Street buildings for centuries and the owners or renters occupied their upper, often residential stories, even today. Very many of such downtowns have been preserved in their original design and have become central attractions for tourism all year around. Oodles of visitors from around the world flood those towns, gaze at Downtown, enjoy their local brand of hospitality, and admire the foresight of the town's government to maintain the pride of their past, even though it does not readily support modern day living expectations.

The commercial-residential building on the right beautifies downtown Dillingen, Bavaria. Almost all houses in that street are representing the baroque style, built in the 17th and 18th century. In this particular house there is a drug store on the ground floor and Dillingen citizens live on the first and second floor in rent.

Some canals in Amsterdam are lined with commercial/residential buildings. Designed gracefully light perhaps as early as the 19th century they still serve their originally intended purposes: they wait on the public in their bottom floors but at the same time maintain residential apartments in their upper floors for well-to-do living.

Houses of dual use in Amsterdam (Website).

Storefronts in Hillsboro Ohio are also of a simpler type, almost as simple as the ones shown for Edinburg, but they still exhibit a graceful roofline and little ornaments on the street-side's house façade, as I have seen in very many rural places in Ohio.

Variations of the venire bricks (2010) and Commercial/Residential Building in Coshocton (2011).

The house in Coshocton shows wall-texture patterns with monochrome-red brick giving the façade a three-dimensional effect as can be seen in many town houses and also in industrial plants of the 19th century. In Germany we called this style the *Railways Gothic* because it coincided with the development of the railways and because most railways-related buildings were fashioned in that style. Accents of white or off-white colored brick or stone seem to be a secondary characteristic favored in Ohio. Since many Ohio towns started within the same few decades of the early 19th century, they use many of the same variations of surface decorations, as is shown in the next photograph of Marysville.

Here are four buildings in one row, all erected most likely within one decade or less. Yet, their facades feature four different styles or hybrids of the Romantic Italianate and Victorian modes, all of them use brick as the main facing material.

Downtown Marysville, 2012.

Immigrants then beautified the centers of many Ohio cities and small towns as they founded them. Only when downtown residents started to abandon the apartments on the residential floors and moved into the more spacious suburbs, and when the commercial businesses vacated the ground floor of those buildings and moved into the strip malls outside of towns, then a slow death of downtown appeared unavoidable.

To combat this trend, the National Park Service of the U.S. Department of the Interior grants tax brakes for the rehabilitating of historic Main Street Commercial Buildings[11], which Congress created in 1976 as incentives to promote historic preservation and community revitalization. Such Federal Government benefits can help individual, private house owners, and developers with the financial burden of renovation. But there still remains the awesome challenge of finding businesses for those buildings that can blossom on Main Street and are not so dependent on customer parking and storage spaces for their goods. Such renovations could, for example, save an Italianate style building that I found in one Ohio Downtown, where the upper loft windows were missing and where, the weather and the pigeons contributed to the decay of the building from top down. That this can be done with good results for the buildings and the economy can be demonstrated in Medina, OH.

Medina in the northern central part of Ohio, in my opinion, maintains the most beautifully downtown I have seen in Ohio so far. There, the intersecting streets East Liberty, North Court, South Court, and West Liberty surround a two acres large, grass-covered center called Town Square, defining the middle of the town.

---

[11] http://www.nps.gov/hps/tps/tax/download/intro_main_street.pdf

Around the town square of Medina, 2012.

The square is framed on three sides by restored commercial-residential houses in the original splendor of the late 19th century. Three county courthouses on the fourth, east side, are well integrated in this town's Town Square. Almost every house front had been renovated, keeping the original ornamental details intact, and perhaps reproducing even the original colors. Every house had different window details and crowns, bracketed cornices, and wall surface materials providing a pleasant variety of façades (as can be seen in the above photograph of one side of the Town Square), and in almost every house the residential floors seemed to be occupied and alive.

On that Wednesday noon, the vehicular traffic was heavy around the square. The stores were open and appealing for comerce, and I saw many visitors. A cozy coffee shop, the Cool Beans Cafe, on the NW corner was busy serving coffee, ice cream, and even small lunches while a dieting class was taught in the back of the room. Marie's Café, an ethnical, Mediterranean-dining place on the N side of the Square, was close by. The parking lot of the United Church of Christ in the NE corner of the Square was filling up with queuing minivans and SUVs of young mothers who were waiting for their little children to be released from pre-school. It must have been many dozens of waiting cars. Jane Ware wrote[12], that the result of renovations around the center starting in 1968: *"are so attractive, that people move to Medina because of the Public Square"*.

Often, a number of stores had been combined in what appears to be one long building block. Sometimes each store determined its own façade style as is also shown in a previous figure depicting a building in Hillsboro. Often, however, the style was uniform within the building block as can be seen in the building on East Main Street in Circleville. Here, the front of the building is vertically divided into three parts accommodating three stores. One of them, the right one, may have maintained the original window treatments on the first residential floor. Most likely, the division goes right through the depth of the entire building, separating the three stores completely, perhaps even with a firewall between them.

Storefront in Circleville, 2012.

[12] Jane Ware, Building Ohio, A Traveler's Guide to Ohio's Rural Architecture, Orange Frazer Press, Wilmington, Ohio, 2002, pp 102-103.

There were a bunch of pigeons lined up on the top of the roof of this house but not on the next buildings. While I took the picture, some flew up, circled around, and settled back on the same roof keeping military style distance between each individual bird. Why would they not extend their resting place onto the neighboring buildings? They looked the same inviting to me. But when I inspected all my Circleville photographs I detected a reason. The immediately neighboring house on the left had a wooden bird sitting on the windowsill of a top window, perhaps simulating a falcon, the archenemy of pigeons.

Pigeons on the roof. See the threat of a Mock falcon, 2012.

During the late morning when the sun had warmed up the town, fife or six Black Vultures circled above downtown. What would they be looking for in this clean and tidy town? Was there a carcass lying in an alley or backyard such as of a dog or cat or even a deer? They were circling for quite some time in repetitive small circles, always using the updraft of the warm air over Main Street to regain height, just above where I was taking pictures. Where they actually scouting? The high noon sun shone through their black wings giving them a bright, silvery color next to their black bodies and against the light blue sky. These big birds might just have enjoyed soaring over Circleville. Perhaps this was their morning exercise and may be they do this often above West Main Street.

Originally, in the early 19th century, Circleville was planned in circles[13] around the county courthouse as its architect-

---

[13] Jane Ware, Building Ohio, A traveler's Guide to Ohio's Rural Architecture, Orange Frazer Press, Wilmington, Ohio, 2002, pp 6-7.

tural center, but a few decades later the circular plans were abandoned for the sake of better commerce and there are now no longer signs of that plan that I could find. Only the vultures lend the town's name some meaning.

A few days later I happened to pass by an interesting church building in Westerville OH. It looked to me as if it was built at the end of the 19th century but it was difficult to get close to it because it was completely enclosed by a construction fence. So I took pictures from a distance and studied those at home.

A New Roman Catholic Church in Westerville, 2011.

With my architectural picture book at hand I tried to determine when exactly it might have been built and what style it was supposed to represent. Then I discovered that it was not being restored at all, as I had thought, but that it was newly constructed with a Romanesque appearance. With the help of the Westerville website I was able to identify the building as the new *St. Paul the Apostle Parish Catholic Church*. How was I fooled so easily? I was unaware that architecture still plans and erects buildings in the fashion of Eclecticism, ignoring subsequent, modern, or contemporary styles, or disallowing architectural novelty development. Perhaps the concept here has some importance for religious buildings where the connection to the past is so important to document both continuity and tradition.

In the next picture I show a church built newly erected during the beginning of the 21st century here in my Worthington neighborhood. It would have been difficult for me to guess at its time of origin if I had not observed its construction.

In summary it seems that American architects of the 19th and beginning 20th century purposefully condensed and squeezed 2000 European years into a potpourri of styles, applied them to American buildings, and then continued to use them even into our time with only minor modifications.

A Brand New Adventist Church in Worthington, built in, 2001.

The current economy collapse begs the question whether the American brands of capitalism and democracy can still secure this country's wellbeing for the immediate future. Ohio should ready itself for a new trust in God as the center of our being and return to a time proven code of morals, evolve economical prince-ples based on that center, place more value in communal welfare, evolve new cultural norms, value governmental services to the community, and design a more fail-safe social safety net that supports the entire population and not only creative entrepreneurs. Out of such a rebirth even novel architectural expressions could truly become unique for North America or even for the world.

Through South & Central Ohio

From a Honda PC 800 pal I received two websites addresses that provide information on scenic motorcycle tours in the US. They are organized by states and include Ohio.[14] The first website suited me best. It shows tours on a Google Map and provides a tiny little description for each. When I searched through the recommendations, I found out that some of those I had already traveled but others I still will have to try. So, I took some and rode them at different weekdays. Because I started to fall in love with the early Ohio downtown appearances, I also took my camera with me to collect pictures of the many interesting little towns that I passed through.

The Beautiful Hocking Hills In Southeast Ohio

One day there was a sudden opening for a motorcycle trip. Gudrun visited with our son Thomas, his wife Katie, and her 2-week old baby Titus, and I was free to pursue my own plans. I had often heard of people taking a long weekend of vacation in the Hocking Hills, the Internet helped me to study about them.

Within this state park are several natural and spectacular features, which are based around rock formations and included: The Old Man's Cave, a narrow, deep gorge featuring waterfalls; Rock house, a rocky area with a rock shelter; Cantwell Cliffs, a broad gorge at the head of a hollow with a unique stone stairway; as well as Ash Cave and Cedar Falls, large rock shelters with waterfalls.

Most of these sights are connected via hiking trails. Even though I was not really planning to hike to any of these exciting sites, I chose Hocking Hills for a welcomed traveling alternative to the otherwise flat central part of Ohio. I was also looking forward to a cool drive on well-shaded roads through wooded hills.

---

[14] www.motorcycleroads.us/states/oh.html and www.motorcycleroads.com

The Hocking Hills area is an hour's worth driving south of Columbus taking SR 33. About halfway south of Lancaster and north of Logan, at Rockbridge, I turned west from US 33 onto SR 374. This small road seemed to me to be the main rout cruising through the beautiful hills on narrow, brand new, perfectly smooth, and well marked blacktop roads. Since it was a Thursday morning, the last one in August, most of the area schools had restarted that week and therefore the park appeared empty; there was no traffic and no visitors to be seen.

When SR 374 met SR 664, I turned north on it where I found a State operated family restaurant. I took lunch in a giant, open dining hall where I sat alone among perhaps more than 100 vacant seats. The food was served via a food bar with unusually many choices of soups, various meets, potatoes, noodles, vegetables, and deserts. There, I eat a soup and rested a short while, then I continued the trip north on SR 664 until it reached US 33 again, a few miles west of Logan, which is the administration seat of Hocking County.

If I had not had a sore back from all the riding, I would have visited Logan also. But my body demanded to get back home, which turned out to be another 90 minutes of tiring, four-lane highway riding. Altogether I covered 181 miles in four hours of riding through Ohio's most beautiful landscape. I felt that I should take the same trip a little later in the season; perhaps in late October when the trees had reached their brightest autumn colors, and takes some photographs then.

State Route 79 In East Central Ohio

Another recommendation was a section of SR 79 in Coshocton County. Starting at Newark, East of Columbus it leads North East where it ends on US 36 near Nellie. It covers 30 miles of a rural road, that meanders through small textured, rural scenery following little streams: first the Wakatomika Creek, then its contributory the Winding Fork, and further North East the Mohawk Creek, which drains into the Walhonding River. The landscape is hilly, with woods and farm crops spreading along the creeks and rolling over many hills. A few tiny settlements are thinly sprinkled along this road.

128

September 4, 2010. Starting my trip in the early forenoon of Saturday I encountered minimal, and apparently only local traffic. Many sections of the road were curvy where the speed was limited to 30 or even 20 miles per hour. The weather was perfect with a temperature in the low seventies. Many brilliant white clouds traveled in the same direction as I did. There were no gasoline stations along the road, no shopping opportunities, and no diners as far as I could ascertain.

Near one little settlement there was a holdup on the road. It may have been where the little Hoover Road joins SR 79, which is called Fallsburg Road NE in this part of Mary Ann Township. Four or five fire engines and ambulances parked on the south side of the road next to two houses. The vehicles blocked the road and held up traffic in both directions. Fire volunteers stood around waiting for something and chatting with each other. One or two police cruisers stood among the vehicles. There was no fire, or car accident, or any other apparent reason for this holdup. Some people sat in lawn chairs in front of the two houses and watched whatever may have been going on. They exhibited calmness in this scene of anticipated emergency.

While I was standing and waiting in a long line of cars with idling engines, I wondered about the lack of organization on one hand, and about the patience of my fellow road users on the other hand. There was no restless horn blowing and no car drivers walking along the road arguing about the holdup. Only the loud music of car radios seemed to help pass the time. Two female rescue workers stood in the middle of the road and looked puzzled as to whether and how they should deal with the growing line of waiting cars on both sides of the holdup.

It was noontime. The sun burned down merciless onto my black helmet and my engine's temperature rose to a high level of discomfort. Eventually, I broke out of the line, inched slowly to the left side of the road and toward these two women. May be, I thought, they can tell me a bypass route; but without even talking to me, they calmly waved me through. I could pass the long line of cuing cars and leave them behind. About 100 yards further down the road in my direction, another fire truck stood at the roadside and filled up with water from a fire hydrant right opposite to the Mary Ann Township Fire department. Had it run out of water?

The rest of the trip was uneventful, except for a little time later when a young man passed by me in a sharp curve, where a double yellow line and a 20 mph sign should have warned him against doing so. His old and noisy Trans Am blasted by me at perhaps more than 70 mph and with screeching tires. He angrily hand-signed at me while passing. When he had passed me he dangerously meandered back and forth from side to side in front of me as if he wanted to show me something, perhaps his anger. What did I do wrong? I did not feel guilty of anything but he reminded me on what my room mate from Edinburgh always said, that "motorcycle riders need to be mindful of crazy drivers sharing the road with them."

Because I ran out of time and, admittedly, was a little jittery from his foolish action, I did not continue on SR 79. At the Goshen Cemetery I turned right (east) onto SR 541, rode it a few miles, and then turned onto SR 60S a fairly straight route toward SR 16 and Dresden. SR 16W brought me back toward home within 90 minutes. The 22 miles on SR 79 were fun to ride and led through beautiful, country. I will gladly ride it again even to its end at Nellie if another opportunity arises.

A Visit to Logan In Hocking County, Southeast Ohio

It was Friday, October 8, and a day that Jonathan could travel with me. Having passed Logan a number of times, we decided on a visit to Logan and then take SR 664 from there, straight up north toward I-70. We left in the morning at 10AM and reached Logan by noon. Logan is a small town of some 7,000 inhabitants. It shares its history with so many other eastern Ohio towns when they blossomed during a period of profitable mining. But then, during the 20th century they all struggled like most other towns in the hills of Eastern Ohio.

1st Presbyterian Church Of Logan (website photo).

We had a little lunch in a downtown café where a few locals, mostly women with children rested from perhaps a morning of shopping or a doctor's visit. From there we spotted an interesting church building on Hunter Street and walked there: The first Presbyterian Church of Logan.

We admired the outside of the building but it did not appear to be open. It says above the central window, that it was built from 1829 until 1897. This is an astonishingly long construction period for a comparatively small building. Designed during the period of Eclecticism it presents a puzzling mix of stylistic revivals where Gothic Revival, Victorian, Eastern Orthodox, and perhaps even some Moorish ideas seem to have contributed to the final outcome. Affected by the long construction period, stylistic preference within the congregation or by the many pastors who served that congregation over those years, might have dictated frequent changes. There may have been changes in the builders or architects. All contributed to a remarkable house of worship. A combination of subdued colors of the main brick, of the ornamental treatment around windows and doors, and of the roof tiles, was in stark contrast to the shouting red of the doors and the rotunda. They did not necessarily match but forced attention of the passersby: "Come by and visit us!"

131

But we wanted to ride on and took SR 664 north. This road promised exciting travel. Over a distance of 22 miles it led straight north and yet, followed many little curves and crossed over dozens of hills and valleys creating a roller coaster effect and constant change of scenery. There was almost no traffic on this early Friday afternoon. When we had come down from the hills on a long downward slope to a junction with SR 312, we overlooked the Raccoon Run valley immediately south of Bremen. Right there a very large cornfield was being harvested by a group of Amish farmers. On some of the field the corn plants had already been cut and the stooks built up to tent-like piles. Perhaps ten flatbed farm wagons in a long line were entering the cornfield. Each wagon was pulled by two Belgian draft horses, and was loaded with the corn stooks.

I marveled at this serene and anachronistic picture of a past time industry, which reminded me of a painting by the American painter Grant Wood.16 From a bird's eye perspective he showed large fields that spread over rolling hills. A horse-drawn plow was only a small spec on that vast spread of acreage. There were no motorized vehicles, both what we observed and what Wood painted. Today's corn harvest is accomplished with huge machines that, while driving over the field on their own power, cut the stooks, separate the corn, and chop the straw for silage. Big trucks come and go to pickup the corn and giant dust clouds emanate from the scene. The artist Grant Wood is well known for another, more famous painting, showing a farmer with a pitchfork, who stands with his wife in front of a farmhouse reminiscent of the Gothic revival.17 Do you remember that picture?

Beyond Bremen, to which we hade paid a special visit at another time, SR 664 passed through the flat country of Richland Township until it ended at SR 256. From there we rode west toward Reynoldsburg, I-70, and home. The entire trip took 5 hours for 152 miles. The weather was beautiful, a shade to cold at the beginning but by noon the thermometer showed 68° F, which was quite pleasant for our driving. In the afternoon on the last stretch toward home a brisk NW wind of 30 mph took a little out of the riding pleasure.

The Hocking Valley Train

For the upcoming Saturday October 30, 2010, a splendid day, with almost guaranteed sunshine and temperatures in the low sixties was predicted. Unlike in the days of my youth, when I often rode in rainy weather, nowadays forecasts are mostly reliable and that is good for us senior hobby riders. Jonathan and I wanted to use this, perhaps last opportunity of the season for an extended motorcycle trip. My youngest son Thomas and his wife Katie with their two small children had planned for a Hocking Valley train-ride. Elsa with her little Hendrik, and my wife Gudrun decided to join them. The Hocking Valley train offers joy rides between Logan and Nelsonville, about 80 miles south of Columbus, along SR 33. Jonathan and I thought to combine their interest and ours. We would ride our motorcycles to the railway station in Nelsonville, eat lunch somewhere on the way, and meet them at the end of their train tour.

As the rode side memorial describes, the Hocking Valley shared its economical up-and-down history with many other settlements of eastern Ohio. The restored train seemed to work well now as a tourist attraction. There were about 100 people on the train when it came into the station, and there were about as many who waited to take the last tour of the day and the season. Jonathan and I took photos of our families arrival and than we left for our own sightseeing trip.

The Hocking Valley Train (AvR, 2010).

When Gudrun and I grew up in Germany, train rides were part of our daily life. Who would ever have thought in those days, that passenger trains, at least in the US, would disappear out of our daily transportation needs, and become a tourist attraction for so many? I wondered where the train company recruited the part time engineers and conductors for this venture. They were personable, friendly, efficient, and punctual just as conductors had been expected to be in the olden days.

Here the family had already debarked and waited for us to take the memorial picture. My wife Gudrun stands on the left, our daughter Elsa (wife of Jonathan) carries her first-born son Hendrik on her arm. Next to her stands our son Thomas with his daughter Lila on his arm and next to him stands his wife Katie with her second child Titus sleeping on her chest. After the photo session, they all walked to their cars and Jonathan and I continued our motorcycle trip

Nellie in Coshocton County, East Central Ohio

As seen on an Ohio map the village of Nellie sits at the eastern end points of SR 715, SR 79, SR 36, and SR 229. Whenever I had planned trips on any of those roads I never reached Nellie because the weather had changed on me or I had ran out of time. Located at the banks of the Walhonding River, Nellie is a very small settlement in the hilly Coshocton County, east of Mt. Vernon and west of I-77. According to the 2000 census, Nellie claims 134 people in 53 households with a median annual per capita income of $15,333.

On Friday, May 20, 2011 the weather forecast for the next day, Saturday indicated sunshine, temperatures around 72°F, and no rain during the daytime. Jonathan called me: he would love a long ride for Saturday and he could start early, he said. I immediately called our new motorcyclist friend Dr. Ted Panhuis, a recently retired veterinarian and BMW motorcycle enthusiast, who had moved into my neighborhood. He agreed to ride with us. Why then should we not complete one of our previous tours and actually reach Nellie OH?

At 8 o'clock in the morning we took SR 3 to Mt. Vernon, which we reached by 9 o'clock. Mount Vernon in Knox County has a population of 16,990 according to the 2010 census. It is the county seat of Knox County.

There is a beautiful town square, as they are so typical for many Ohio towns. A memorial column reaches out of its middle. A number of state and county routes meet there and spread out again from there. Close by we found a place that would serve us coffee at this early hour of the day. The *Sips Coffee and Bakery* sits at the junction of S. Main Street and Vine Street. The shop occupies the entire lower floor of a very large merchants building which may have been built around the beginning of the 20th century and which had been restored very tastefully maintaining a hint of its original Italianate style.

We parked our motorcycles opposite the shop entrance and I was sent to scout out the shop offerings. On the right side of this picture stands Jonathan (the taller figure) conversing with Ted (with the white head) while they waited for my verdict.

Our motorcycles parked in front of the Sip Coffee.

While we enjoyed the coffee and the pleasant, old-fashioned small-town atmosphere of the place, Ted told us a little about himself, how he as an eleven-year-old boy had emigrated with his parents from the Netherlands into the US. He finished school in this country, received his veterinary degree at The Ohio State University, and then practiced small animal medicine in the Cleveland area for forty years. At the beginning of 2011 he retired to Worthington where his two married daughters live. He owns several motorcycles and, he said, he loves long riding tours.

Refreshed from the coffee and the discussions, we continued our trip on SR 36E with the plan to eat lunch in Nellie. That trip took 90 minutes at comfortable speeds that allowed us to observe the beautifully rolling hill country while we were flying by. There were only very few, tiny little settlements along the way and there was little traffic to mind.

The weather was kind to us; the temperature stayed in the high sixties, and a grey overcast cleared slowly. We saw many vultures and buzzards circling above us in search for pray, or perhaps they enjoyed their flight just as we did our ride. Traveling as a team of three took a little more effort to watch out for each other and to stay together, but in my mind, it increased the fun greatly. Both, Jonathan on his 1984 BMW R80 and Ted on his 2008 BMW R1200 were diligent, attentive, and deliberately proactive riders in spite of the potentials of their sporty and powerful motorcycles. We kept a safe distance of several car lengths between us to increase the personal safety margin, which also allowed us more attention to the countryside.

When we descended from the hills down to the Walhonding River, we reached Nellie closely built to the riverbanks. But the village was so small that we could not even determine a village center nor see something resembling a restaurant. The next settlement, Coshocton was only 10 miles further down the Walhonding River where it joins the Tuscarawas River to form the Muskingum River. So we decided to ride on to there. We saw many tourists' cars in the parking lot of Roscoe Village at the northern edge of Coshocton, which is a nice touristic place where one can learn about the historical influence that man-made canals had on the early Ohio economy. However, we did not stop there; we rode into Coshocton to find a place to eat lunch.

136

Coshocton is a small city, and yet, we were so familiar with her name because it is mentioned daily on Public Radio hosting one of its radio stations. A little green square forms her center with the county's beautifully styled courthouse in its middle. Two or three streets around the center represent the business center, which was well cared for. And yet, in spite of two electric power plants in Coshocton's imme- diate vicinity, she had seemingly lost some of her charm and wealth of earlier times. Still, we found a few beautiful merchant houses built at the turn of the 19th century telling of better past times.

One building caught my eye especially because its very clean façade which was faced with a veneer of concrete blocks or plates casted in classical decorative patterns. I had already seen this construction technique for bank buildings in other Ohio towns such as Delaware, Marysville, and Cadiz. It seemed to me that concrete, the new construction material of those days was applied there to imitate surface ornamentation (called "textile block system") of past building styles. Surely this construction method simplified and reduced the fabrication costs of previous centuries where such decorative patterns were hewn in marble or fashioned in other masonry. It also facilitated easier mass production of these plates. The façade achieved a light and very uniform grey color and was very clean but had a rough-to-the-touch surface appea- rance in the sunlight, very, different to grey marble or limestone. The texture was a little too painstakingly geometric for my taste.

Decades later the mechanical properties of concrete (even enforced with steel) facilitated novel construction techniques and in the 1890s high risers were born then.

Near the courthouse we found an old style eatery appealing to our taste. Although it was noon, there were only two or three tables occupied within a large room that could easily fill 40 tables. The wall decorations were reminiscent of the fifties. The service was efficient and fast.

At first, Ted and I had ordered a "German Bologna Sandwich" and we both made fun of the interesting mix of culinary terms of origin? What is so German about Bologna sandwiches? Bologna sausage is an American sausage derived from and somewhat similar to the Italian mortadella (a finely hashed/ground pork sausage containing cubes of lard; it originated in the Italian city of Bologna). Perhaps "German" refers to "sandwich", but German sandwiches are normally made with firm slices of rye bread and not usually covered with mayonnaise and mixtures of meet, cheese, and salad leaves, as is often the case for good tasting, American sandwiches. So, why are they not called American sandwiches? But then all of these semantics did not really matter. We had to change our order anyway since the eatery was fresh out of Bologna sausage. So we ordered a Reuben sandwich on rye bread instead. Reuben is a Hebrew name and may imply a Jewish origin of this rather popular sandwich, which contains corned beef on sauerkraut. It turned out to taste deliciously and would be worthy of an American name.

While we were eating, we planned our return trip to follow SR 541, which would lead us west, from Coshocton to Martinsburg where it would change into SR 62, bring us further west toward SR 161, and home from there.

Jonathan and I had taken SR 541 before and its beauty fascinated us again. It led over the tops of hills, through prairie-like, tree-less areas, much of it untouched by larger settlements, crop farming, or cattle ranching, and leading along a game reservation on its north side. When we had traveled that road earlier this year we should have patented that route for its biking beauty. This time, many motorcycle groups passed us there and they could have already provided us with royalty income since they obviously liked what we had discovered. This first pretty day after many days of rain had brought them out onto the road just like us. But, aside from kidding, can we actually patent the use of beautiful roads?

We saw local people along the way tending their flower patches or cutting their lawns. Many houses were surrounded by literally acres of manicured lawns. Most of the mowing was done by women who made their rounds across the grassy fields while sitting on little riding mowers. Where were the men? Did they have to work for income, or did they watch Saturday games on television, or were they touring the country on their motorcycles? Regardless, I enjoyed seeing the neatly trimmed lawns and gorgeous flowerbeds that surrounded the houses along the roadside.

The entire trip, including two breaks, took six hours, and we covered 140 miles of some of Ohio's most appealing landscapes.

My Most Exciting Tour in Ohio

When my oldest son Derik returned to his home base in Hawaii from a one-year Iraq deployment, he and his family came to visit us in Worthington for a few vacation days. Derik, an officer in the US Army had always had a love for motorcycle riding and he used to own Harley-Davidson (H&D) bikes throughhout his military career. Therefore my son in-law Jonathan suggested for us to take a bike trip together. Our neighbor Ted Panhuis also agreed to join us. From a used-bike dealer in the very south of Columbus we rented a 07 H&D Street Glide for Derik. The bike was in excellent mechanical condition and quite attractive in its deep blue color.

Derik with a rented 07 H&D Street Glide, 2011.

What would be an exciting tour in Ohio for someone from an evergreen Hawaii who had just returned from deployment in Iraq's desert lands? Would the lush Amish country be attractive to him? Because of the great initial distance to get there I was a little worried with that choice. There would be an 80 miles or 90 minute ride to the center of Amish country and an equivalent length of time to get back home from there without having toured Amish country yet. Also the weather predictions were not so promising with temperatures anticipated around 100° F, high humidity, and a 20% likelihood of thunderstorms. But since Derik was coming regardless of the weather expectations, since the bike was rented, and because nobody else of the team was worried, we dared the trip. In order to get the first and dull part of the trip out of the way, we started at 7AM when it was not that hot yet, but there was thick fog along US 62 until we reached Millersburg in Holmes County. There the sun broke through and the fog dissipated in the air.

From there we started the actual tour through the Amish's Holms County. On our first branch we rode from Millersburg to Mt. Hope, had a nice breakfast there in the local Mennonite restaurant, and then visited the weekly farmers' market right next to the restaurant. This event became the highpoint of our entire trip. The Mt. Hope Auction serves the local farming community and offers anything even remotely farm related from garage sale kitsch to building supplies, all kinds of farm implements, farm animals, farm products, and even guns for sale. In the burning heat of 100° F, we saw about 70 buggies with their horses tied to the perimeter fence around the auction property. They were neatly lined up just like modern cars parked next to a shopping mall. There were hundreds of local farmers, Amish and non-Amish customers with their families to buy, trade or sell. There were also a few tourists trying to find some precious objects as reminders of their Amish country visit, or just watching the spectacle just as we did.

Ted, the other retired veterinarian of our travel team took a picture (right lower corner) of the buggy lineup. He was as excited as I had always been with all these horses in harness, and buggies. Slowly we meandered through the crowds and watched some of the ongoing activities. In one corner of the area an auction of hay proceeded and we stood for a while to watch the people there and listen to them.

140

At another site, crates were piled up for later auctioning and they contained pigeons, poultry chicks, and young rabbits.

Amish Buggies Parked, Mt. Hope Farmers' Market, 2011.

Although the auctioneers spoke English, most of the Amish, as they could easily be identified by their traditional dress, conversed in their own language. The Holms County Amish have their European origin in the German speaking part of Switzerland of the 18th century. Hearing their Alemannic dialect has always warmed my heart since its intonation or "music" is so close to that of my home dialect of Southwestern Germany. I said the "music", because although the sentence melody is so familiar to me, many of the words are so different that I cannot really understand much of what is said. Some of these words I recognize from my own home dialect. For example they use the word "Gaul" for the horse, just as I knew it, whereas the High German word is "Pferd", which is used by German speakers of today. But most of their other words especially nouns I do not recognize. And still, I get a warm feeling of sympathy when I hear them talk.

On our second branch we continued our trip southward to Berlin. The short road to there, Co R 77 appeared like a main Amish highway. An almost endless line of buggies traveled both ways. Elegant horses of the Standard Bred type trotted with ease along the road and pulled buggies that were filled to the rim with Amish families. To avoid that the noise of our motorcycles (especially Derik's rented H&D) would spook one or the other of these horses we passed by them slowly and with great respect. But it seemed that these horses were well trained and accustomed to traffic noise around them.

141

In Berlin we strolled through the main street's shopping area. This weekday morning there was not much tourism yet. We saw mostly Amish or Mennonite local people coming to work there or delivering goods to the stores. The last time we were here, Jonathan and I had to warm up from a very cold arrival; this time, the great heat and humidity urged us eventually to move on.

The third branch of our trip brought us back to Millersburg. I had selected some little township roads to get there in the hope that we would see people working around their farms but it seemed they were all attending the farmers' market. In Millersburg we stopped to eat lunch at a nice downtown hotel in which we had eaten already some years earlier. The food was good and the air conditioning cooled us down nicely, actually holding us a little longer than would have been necessary for eating lunch. Satisfied with the ride and the things we had seen, we then headed home on US 62.

The entire tour took seven hours and covered 188 miles, and when we arrived back home we were filled with wonderful impressions of Ohio but were also exhausted from the long ride and the merciless heat.

Nowadays, when I am asked what to recommend as the most impressive and perhaps even unique place for sightseeing in Ohio, I have no hesitation to recommend Holms County first, preferably to be visited on a Wednesday before noon to experience the Farmers' market in Mt. Hope. Not only is Holms County located within a beautiful landscape, but even more so because it allows a glimpse into Amish life of today. I personally consider Holms County as a good demonstration of religious and cultural tolerance as they have formed the American civilization, a demonstration of peace and harmony at a time when other parts of the world are in bloody war and uprising over the very same issues, namely whether or how different religions or cultures can or cannot exist next to each other, and how they can benefit from each other. I am convinced that the USA will find a similar, peaceful way to assimilate today's large immigration waves such as for example cultural Roman Catholics from Middle and South America, and Moslems from the Near East and Africa, without regarding them as a threat to our way of life. They will, and are already filling niches in our workforce that current citizen have little incentive to fill.

Bike Review And Modification
The Solo bike

By now, I have ridden the Honda Pacific Coast 800 for eighteen months and 8,000 miles. The purchase price that I had paid for the bike did not really reflect the excellent condition of this 21-year old motorcycle. Its exterior was in mint condition and its mechanical underpinnings were functioning flawlessly. It was built in 1989 as one of the first batch of this model sold in the USA. It had only an odometer reading of 11,840 miles. Since the instrument panel functioned properly, there was no good reason to doubt the shown mileage. So I always wondered why the price, not only of this particular bike, but of all used PC 800 bikes was so low compared to other bikes of that size? It could not possibly be an indicator of the quality of that make because I heard only good things about the PC800 and the web does not offer any advice on repairs, as can be found in abundance for BMW bikes. Since I am not the usual type of motorcycle rider, I knew of no good reasons for this low price. Perhaps the paradigm of its design did not meet the ideals of the ever growing number of American motorcycle enthusiast who are attracted to power boasting engines reminiscent of the motorcycle hay-days of long gone times; or the racing junkies who cater to fast, technical wonder motorcycles that compete with the fastest on roads and off-road tracks.

The PC 800 was designed for the white color, well to do urbanite on the American West Coast, who like me would use it occasionally to ride to work or tour the countryside on sunny days for pure enjoyment. It was to be a sturdy bike. When I looked up "sturdy" the following synonyms were listed: "strong"-which it certainly is, "powerful" - which it is, and "well-built" - which it undeniably is. This bike model was to provide just enough power to compete well in the traffic with today's cars.

Its operation was to be simple without fancy adjunct mechanisms but very comfortable, almost like a bigger scooter. The driver was to ride upright and master the bike with ease while dressed in good clothes but not get dirty. The mechanical under-pinnings were designed to require a bare minimum of regular maintenance. The entire bike was encased in a fairing that keeps road dirt from its interior, and unskilled hands from fiddling with its mechanics. An occasional down spraying with water was enough to keep it clean and presentable. The fairing consisted of a cleverly designed series of polymer panels. They were lightweight with a good mix of stiffness and flexibility (if I knew a word for this material property, I would have used it). The panel edges fit into each other with ridges and grooves. At strategic places little tabs locked one panel into the next to avoid sliding, rattling, or dislodging. Some of the panels were also to be fastened to the bike's frame or engine block with screws or rubber pegs. When assembled in place, the whole fairing functioned like Tupperware encasement, locking its parts together with press fit to maintain form stability. This encasement was extremely stable and, when installed properly, was free of vibration-generated noises such as rattling or groaning, and there were no externally visible screw heads or other fasteners allowing for clues how the fairing stayed in place.

Another design feature may have been to offer no additional, ancillary devises or beautifications, as they are so popular for many other bike makes. In fact there are not even places on the bike to attach things such as for example additional lights. The whole design concept of the bike appealed to me at this time of my life: *Always be ready and fit for a comfortable ride*. This turned out to be true for me during the past 18 months. The motorbike was always ready to go for a trip. But as to the American public, the majority of envisioned customers were not attracted to this bike, belittling it as a "scooter". So it did not sell well and its production was eventually terminated in 1998, only a short nine years after it came onto the US market. Since the frame and drivetrain have been continued in subsequent models with sportier, more traditional motorcycle appearances, I surmise with disappointment, that not enough gentlemen were interested in riding comfortable bikes. May be they leaned more towards comfortable sports cars?

Since this bike had been ridden about 12,000 miles before I owned it, and since I knew nothing of its past maintenance history, I replaced the spark plugs, even though they might not really have need it and I also exchanged all fluids just to be on the safe side. The battery looked like the original one of 1989. So, I removed it and had it tested: it was found to be in good condition and actually lasted for another two years. The tire profiles still had some good life on them and so I had left them in place also. The brake pads were in good condition and needed no replacement. But all these little procedures, that have never required more than an hour or two on my previous bikes; here, with the fairing in place, they demanded a day's worth of unwrapping the bike before I could actually do service procedures. For example, the battery, which in other bikes is easily accessible under the seat, in my PC 800 bike, however, all panel sheets on the right side needed to be removed to reach it under the seat. Similarly, to exchange the spark plugs, the side panels on both sides of the bike needed to be removed. Checking the disk brakes of the front wheel required the removal of the mudguard panels, taking another hour of work for the unskilled (company-envisioned) gentlemen owner.

The Honda PC 800 in Complete "Tupperware" Encasing (Web Site).

Although Honda provided a good description of panel removal, it still took me a long time to figure out how to remove one panel after the other without breaking the panels or their interlocking tabs. So, some tabs broke off, but with time I got better in judging how much or little force was needed to remove or re-install the panels without inflicting damage. Interestingly, every time I had to do this, I ended up with some leftover nuts or bolts and no apparent places to put them. I now keep a little plastic zip-lock bag filled with those that are still looking for their designated place. But all in all, I think I have become better and faster in removing and replacing the fairing for any and all small maintenance procedures.

Some times, I have been thinking, it would have been best to buy first a PC 800 to learn all the necessary procedures for routine maintenance — how ever few there may be needed to maintain the bike in good condition. Then, when I would be ready to do the procedures well and without damage to the fairing, then I should buy a second PC 800 for enjoying the bike optimally. Perhaps I should do that in my next life. In this one, I am actually happy and satisfied with my first PC 800, so far at least.

The Trike

Another aspect to the bike however emerged recently that needed a solution soon. The bike weighed a whopping 650 lbs., to which I became increasingly aware every time the bike came to a stand at traffic lights, when I wanted to mount or de-mount it, or when I needed to push it in reverse into the bike shed. My legs had become too week to hold it safely upright. In recent days I dropped it twice while trying to mount it. This was not a problem with my former BMW rig since it had the sidecar wheel to keep it upright. I would have to quit riding motorcycles altogether if there were no solutions available.

My friends offered lots of good advice: "Buy a smaller bike or even better, a scooter", they said. "It now comes with engines up to 650 cc." "It could be less heavy and your feet would be closer to the ground". "It can come with two additional wheels either in the back or the front to keep it upright". "Look into the Can-Am Spyder, a trike designed with two wheels in the front and a single, powered one in the back". Consider one of the big trikes of Harley-Davidson or Honda Goldwing that were modified to have two powered wheels in the back." I looked up all these possibilities on the web and they could be exciting opportunities for me, solving my balance problems, but they had price tags for either new or used models between $14,000 and $35,000. This would be too high a price for the few more riding years the Lord may grant me.

Then I saw on the Internet a PC 800 just like mine with a neat little sidecar attached to it which was for sale for $4,000. I was excited: this could be my third sidecar. I called but the seller had already sold it. He offered, however, to rig up my bike with another sidecar. But then I saw another PC 800 just like mine but with two (non-powered) wheels added to the back and I liked that idea even better. Tow-Pack manufactured such wheels for many bike models, including the PC 800. I called and InstaTrike, would sell them to me while a motorcycle shop in Medina OH would attach them to my bike. The total cost would be less than $4,000, without a need to buy another vehicle or to sell mine. The InstaTrike wheels were described to require no modifications on the bike and could be removed or re-attached within minutes if needed. So I decided for that solution which, God willing, could allow me another few years of site seeing in Ohio from the top of my bike.

On Tuesday thereafter, the trike wheels had arrived with the service people in Medina OH. On Wednesday morning I drove to Medina where Blackburn's Trikes operated a nice, clean, little motorcycle shop. By noon I could ride the new trike back home.

The trip home was a 90 miles ride on Interstate-71 and it gave me two hours time to get used to the riding peculiarities of a trike. Had I not had sidecar experience before, I would have been totally disappointed with the trike right away. The exciting sporty feel of a solo-bike soaring along the road was gone. The two extra wheels in the back held me down to the road, let me feel all street bumps, exaggerated the vibration of the engine, and forced me to steer exclusively with the steering bar. That required pulling on one side and pushing on the other of the bar with iron determination and strong force. The trike, just like my rigs, had the strong tendency to change direction with unevenness of the road or with strong side winds, and I had to counter-steer forcefully to keep the intended riding direction. Cues, which the bike offered to change the driving direction, would have been misleading if followed: Shifting weight and leaning would not have changed driving direction as they do in a solo bike but create dangerous situations. Those cues needed to be ignored. Since most paved roads today have a gentle slope to the edge of the road called crowning, the trike pulled to the right whenever I rode on the curbside lane – all the 90 miles - until I got used to this peculiar behavior again. Also, turning into a curve by means of the steering bar created the sensation that the bike lifts up on the centrifugal side, and it probably does. That feeling had to be re-experienced and counteracted with renewed body reflexes.

With some trips around town, I adjusted slowly to this new riding experience and at the same time I started to appreciate the new assurance that I could leave my feet on the footrests when stopping. I needed not fear anymore, that the bike might topple down under me. That was the reason why I turned to a trike in the first place. What a great relieve it was now that I had made this choice.

Motor-tricycle (Trike), 2011.

In a way, the bike's behavior with training wheels was very similar to that of a rig, except even harder to steer. Once, I asked a bike technician who owned a trike with the bike's rear wheel removed and with the two rear wheels of the trike motorized, whether he had the same steering difficulties I have and he said: "Yes."

Years later the bike's rear wheel had a puncture hole. Although I tried to plug it, the hole was too big to be closed even with many plugs. I was also advised that a tire with a plug would never be safe and I needed a new tire. Since I was no longer able to change the tire myself, I needed to remove the training wheels, load the bike onto a trailer and bring it to the Honda service shop. When the tire was replaced, I drove the bike home in its two-wheel configuration. I was thrilled how easy and sporty it rode without the training wheels. Steering by weight shifting was still part of my automatic responses—I did not need to think about it. It was sad, to reattach the wheels, but it was necessary for my safety while riding the bike for another few years, God willing.

What Will Ohio Be Tomorrow?

The Ohio I have traveled and learned to enjoy has mostly been its portion of the Appalachians in the south and east of the state. That region resembled most closely the picturesque landscape of southwestern Germany where I grew up and where I spent my youth hiking, camping, hitchhiking, bicycling, and moped riding. That German hill country had been farmed ever since the Germanic immigrants started to cultivate it systematically during the 3rd century AD. In contrast, the Appalachians that I have seen until now has been farmed for not much longer than 200 years and, at least today it does not give the impression of a rich farm or forestland. Its settlements are generally small, the farms are thinly dispersed over the hills and valleys, and, with the exception of some larger crop farms in bottomlands, are very small. So again, I had to go back and study the history of this area in order to gain an appreciation of what happened there during the past 200 years and how that history shaped the land and the people of today.

I learned that farmers in the Appalachians of Ohio came predominately from east Tennessee, eastern Kentucky, and western Virginia and settled during the late 18th and the beginning of the 19th centuries. Their forefathers were immigrants from the British borderlands between northern England and southern Scotland, and their earlier displacement to Ulster, Ireland. They had brought their folkways with them, shaping the culture and politics of the Appalachians still today[15]. Their small farms were diversified and designed to provide mainly for their own family needs. But from the late 19th century through most of the 20th century, official reports describe, that much of that land had then been *"exploited by absentee owners of extractive industries. Many parts of the region were completely transformed by the coming of timber, coal, gas, oil, and clay extracting industries in the 1870s.*

---

[15] David Hackett Fischer, Albion's Seed, four British Folkways in America, Oxford University Press, New York, 1991.

Numerous Americans were enriched by the exploitation of Appa-lachian natural resources and cheap labor, while Appala-chians themselves became one of the most politically disfranchised and poor groups of people in the Global North."[16] By today, most of these industries are gone and have left behind a land that is depri-ved of its resources, especially forest and fertile soil, and robbed of future profitable farming. Most of the original, small farms in the hills are no longer self-sustaining and need to seek additional income.

This unchecked overuse of the land also occurred in many other countries and is still practiced in many. I am thinking of countries of the former Soviet Union and of China. It is astounding to me that the US government was not willing enough or able to protect its land and agriculture by regulating against such greedy and devastating exploitation. Perhaps the strong believe of the local people in self-reliance and resistance to federal government involvement is to blame in part. I have often marveled whether the USA brand of democracy and capitalism, with its seemingly limitless freedom tolerated for prospering individuals, has been the right political system to preserve the land for its perpetual use by all of its citizens? Have the federal and local governments learned from those exploitive practices of the past and can they now make better decisions when they consider permits for the advanced drilling technique called hydraulic fractioning to mine natural gas and oil? Has that form of government been suitable for the pursuit of long-range goals even when they require expensive investments in the short run? Interesting is also, that long range considerations were not debated by the presidential candidates of the election campaigns of 2012.

I do not know what could help the economy of today's Appalachia, but the beauty of her landscape and her remote little towns are yearning for tourism. On my many trips through that area of the past four years, I observed some tourists such as retirees in their search for yet undiscovered, valuable antiques, and of late even flocks of motorcycle riders crossing the Appalachian country roads on weekends. I have seen promotion of hospitality by local merchants and governments. But their efforts should be supported in a bigger way by other parts of Ohio, those, which

---

[16] Appalachian Ohio, from Wikipedia, 2011.

have good local economies and for whose citizens, local tourism might become more desirable at a time when the world's economy suffers and when large vacation trips have given way to local vacation alternatives.

Of course tourism is a seasonal business and cannot feed all of the inhabitants of the Appalachians throughout the entire year, but it should provide a worthwhile, additional income for many. Here are some examples: During the past 5 years I often drove with my BMW rig to the small settlement of Lithopolis, next to the town of Canal Winchester. Lithopolis appeared to me as if it had been forgotten 50 years ago or longer. But in that little place was a BMW Motorcycle store. It specialized in used replacement parts and refurbishing classical BMW motorcycles. Because I often needed such parts, I visited the store often. The people there were always helpful and personable. The store had the peculiar name of *Re-Psycle* and I often wondered, why on earth it would settle for Lithopolis, 30 miles from the metropolis of Columbus, while the tiny Lithopolis itself might not have a single potential customer? One day, I asked the owner Mark Seidle, what his reasons were and he replied that 90 percent of his business was in mail ordering and that he could reside anywhere, but liked Lithopolis. That particular day, after shopping there with Jonathan, we rode into the village to find a place for a cup of coffee. There was only one downtown street in Lithopolis, and we were amazed to see that that E. Columbus Street had just been re-surfaced, sidewalks had been added, the few commercial/residential houses — may be ten of them in all — had been restored, and flowers were planted everywhere along the sidewalks. A coffee place was in one of the historical houses. Its owner had picked a German theme for the store and had named it *"Das KaffeeHaüs von Frau Burkhart"*. Large, black & white photo prints of German towns decorated the inside walls. The baked goods had a German appearance and German named "Kaffee" was served. We spent a relaxing half hour there before we headed home again. Perhaps more Re-Psycle customers will now stop there.

With the re-appearance of recreational motor biking on the roads, and the many events motorcycle or bicycle clubs are having, I could imagine — as an example — bikers' meetings in McConnelsville where they could help celebrate Ohio's history as part of their agenda. They could bring in hundreds of bikers for a prolonged weekend who may purchase gasoline there, eat in the downtown's only restaurant, and may even rent a meeting site and overnight accommodations. They might plan this regularly perhaps even annually such as the draft horse fanciers do in Fawcett south of Peebles. They might celebrate Indian history on Serpent Mound and camp there for a weekend. They might assemble in Marietta or Portsmouth in commemoration of their significant contributions to the birth of the state. They might enjoy Ohio just as I have since I moved to Columbus with my family in 1997. People in Columbus then told me that Ohio would grow on me, and it really did.

In upcoming years I might want to explore the lowlands of northern and western Ohio, which I was told, were settled by a set of different immigrants who came from the New England area of Puritan stock, who exhibit a different philosophy of using their land, engaging their government, coping with the changing times and fortunes, and exhibiting their more social culture. All I need to hope for is that I can continue to control a bike that reliably brings me to some of the places that I would love to visit.

P.S.

In March 2013 my natural but arthritic left hip joint was replaced. During the subsequent nine months of recovery, it became painfully clear that I had reached the end of my motor-cycle hobby, and that I should sell it. An 82 years old man from the south of Columbus came to look at it. He was mainly interested in the bike's radio and when I confirmed that the radio works fine, he bought the bike. His son came along saying that the trike setup was just perfect for his father.

A little scooter will allow me now to get around in Columbus's immediate vicinity; perhaps it will also help me wean off from the wonderful big bikes.

The End

Table of Contents

www.ingramcontent.com/pod-product-compliance
Lightning Source LLC
Chambersburg PA
CBHW060346090426
42734CB00011B/2059